THE OLYMPIAN
FROM SEOUL TO SALVATION

THE TRUE STORY OF OLYMPIC BOXER JAMIE PAGENDAM

BY JAMIE PAGENDAM JR

WITH JAMIE PAGENDAM & STEVE PAGENDAM

THE OLYMPIAN:
FROM SEOUL TO SALVATION

Written by Jamie Pagendam Jr
with Olympic Boxers Jamie Pagendam and Steve Pagendam

This book is a creative non-fiction depicting the real life
recollections and memories of Jamie Pagendam and Steve Pagendam.
Some of the dialogue has been recreated based on these recollections.

TABLE OF CONTENTS

ACKNOWLEDGEMENTS

Jamie Pagendam Jr.
The Author of: The Olympian: From Seoul to Salvation

It was an amazing honor to write this book. I'd like to thank my uncle and dad for believing in me and entrusting me to do their story justice. I have never felt this type of fulfillment or satisfaction with a piece of work before, so I appreciate getting to take on this project with freedom and trust. This experience has inspired me to be unapologetically myself and always strive to live creatively.

Thank you to my brother Brad. I owe a lot of my creativeness and my love of the arts to you. The most creative person I know. I've learned so much from you, but most importantly to be kind, loving and positive.

Thank you to my sister Aimie for your unconditional support. You are a continuous inspiration. Never give up on your dreams, because music lives forever inside of you.

Thanks to my brother Jon. I can truly say you are my one true rock. Your opinion means so much to me. I know where to go when I need help and when I need to feel safe. You have no idea how important you have been.

Thank you to my mom. The greatest person I've ever known and ever will know. Thank you for always encouraging creativity and letting me be weird and different. She loved to read and always wanted to write a book, and I truly believe we wrote this book together. I love you.

I dedicate this book to my mother, Debbie Pagendam. xo

ACKNOWLEDGEMENTS

Jamie Pagendam
1988 Canadian Olympian in Boxing

This book is dedicated to all the people who have supported and touched my life in ways I can't begin to describe. To say I did this on my own would be completely false. I owe a lot to my friends and family who have been an incredible source of encouragement and inspiration.

My wife, Franny, for the years of support and love, and for understanding my need to succeed and never leave anything unfinished.

My brother Steve for making me realize the true meaning of life and God's gift. Your encouragement through the years of my transition from boy to man cannot go unmentioned. Your unending support in everything I did will never be forgotten.

My children, Tanner and Victoria, for always believing in me and cheering me on. You guys give me the focus, drive and determination to be a better person.

To my nephew, Jamie Jr., who, through his words and wisdom, captured the emotional roller coaster of my life and put it into the creation of this book.

To my mother and father for the love and nurturing they provided which shaped me into the person I am today.

To my most loyal friend, Barry Stubbert. From childhood to present, you have always supported and understood my dreams. Thanks for never questioning me in choosing boxing over hockey.

ACKNOWLEDGEMENTS

Jamie Pagendam
1988 Canadian Olympian in Boxing.. continued

Hank Boone took me under his wing as an 11-year-old kid and pushed me to be the best I could be. Thank you for showing me the true sport of boxing and spending countless hours in the gym with me.

I'd also like to thank Roofus Johnson for his technical teachings and skill development. Vinnie and Val Ryan for always having my best interests at heart and helping me achieve my Olympic dream. Ray Napper Sr. who welcomed me into his club in 1988 and supported my Olympic goal.

Thanks to Vernon McGriff who was my greatest rival in boxing and one of U.S.A.'s best amateur boxers. You brought out the very best in me and helped me mature as a fighter.

Special thanks to Theresa Jacobs. You gathered and organized the facts and timelines which assisted in getting the ball rolling.

Shout out to the past and present members of the St. Catharines Boxing Club for your continued contributions to the great sport of boxing.

And most importantly, I want to acknowledge Jesus Christ my Lord and Savior as none of this would have been possible without him in my life.

Phillipians 4:13
For I can do everything God asked me to, with the help of Christ who gives me the strength and power

THE OLYMPIAN:

FROM SEOUL TO SALVATION

CHAPTER I
DeLorean

Another day goes by as I work in this dark, dingy factory known as Hayes Dana. It's a job, it makes me money, but there are so many other places I'd prefer to be. As I work the factory line, my mind is moving at an unsettling pace. I don't know if the ringing in my ears is from the years of getting hit in the head over and over, or if it's simply from the loud machinery I'm surrounded by on a daily basis. Either way, I'm used to it now. I've become used to a lot of things as I've gotten older.

I feel more vulnerable, which was never an issue in my youth. When I look back at it now, I realize I didn't fear anybody—or at least, that's what I tried to portray. But you know, the longer you pretend to be something, the more likely you are to embody that trait and make it part of yourself. Damn, I used to be a cocky little prick. But it worked for the lifestyle I was living. Nobody messed with Jamie Pagendam; they knew what I was capable of.

I was a tough kid. One time, I was walking home from school and saw a group of older kids hovering over my brother, Steve, knocking him around. I dropped my bag and sprinted as fast as I could to them. Steve saw me in top flight, making my way toward what was actually just a group of his friends wrestling around for fun. He tried to wave me off, but I was already locked in on my targets. Despite the obvious size difference, I knocked a few of them over before Steve was able to scoop me up and explain the situation. It had looked like they were fighting, and I always had my brother's back. We had a strong, tight-knit relationship. The Pagendam boys laughed together, fought together and showed much love for one another.

The name Pagendam was well respected in our hometown of St. Catharines and the cities closely surrounding it. Even to this day, anyone who was an adult during our rise to athletic notoriety will know the name Pagendam and what it represents. And many of them know what that name could have become.

All those years of hard training, dedication and success has led me to a punch-in clock at 6:30 a.m. I remember all the hard hours of sparring and running up and down hills, preparing for the next big fight. I used to shower in the downstairs part of the boxing gym alongside my training partners. Now, I share a locker room with men who are working here for the same reason I am: We didn't go to college, but we have to feed our families.

It's not the worst job in the world, but I had much bigger plans for myself. As I wipe the sweat off my brow, it's mixed with the scent of oil and metal. My arms glisten, soaked in my own sweat. This once was a thing to feel great pride in. The difference being that instead of smelling oil and machinery, it was the beautiful smell of leather, tape and competition. I can hear my gloves bouncing off the heavy bag as I snap a three-punch combination into the core of the bag. I can hear my gloves snapping into the ribcage of an opponent as I deliver one of my classic hooks to the body. I can also hear them slapping against the wall as I whip them across the locker room after a disappointing loss.

Even though it's been fifteen years, these thoughts still own my mind. It may sound nice to reminisce about the good ol' days, but they are way behind me. The good memories are fine, but they remind me of all the bad times too. Unfortunately, as time has passed, the bad memories have seemingly outweighed the good. The fact that I haven't been able to get past these dark memories is long overdue. The what-if's and the if-only's are constantly feeding through my brain, making my heart beat faster with every additional thought.

I can't even call it regret, because I had no control over the matter. People I thought I could trust let me down that day. With no apologies ever given, how can they receive forgiveness? Do they lay awake at night with the same thoughts I'm imprisoned with? I'm not saying I don't forgive those involved, but it'd be much easier to offer forgiveness if they could at first admit they were wrong and extend some sort of apology. I have no closure, and at this point, I don't see it ever being fully resolved.

These days, boxing doesn't even seem to be my biggest problem. I think it's safe to say that everything I feel, every negative thought I have, stems from how my boxing career unfolded. Not just the physical toll it took, but the mental aftermath I was forced to bathe in for years after. I feel used. I feel betrayed. I feel constantly under the microscope.

As I stand staring blankly ahead of me, my current thoughts are interrupted; I get a slap on the back of my shoulder. My supervisor yells in my ear to get my head out of the clouds and get back to work. However, he didn't say it quite that kindly. I put my head down, slightly embarrassed. This sucks. Now I know all the other workers are staring me down, wondering what's wrong with me. I wish I could just leave this place and never come back; I'm beyond overwhelmed. I'd be lying if I said this doesn't happen often. Maybe if everyone would just mind their own damn business.

It's felt like no matter where I go, whether it's working in the Thorold Tunnel, here at Hayes Dana or even just out in public, people are giving me side eye. It's scary to have people want to punch your lights out. It's even scarier not knowing what people are saying about you behind your back. I can handle myself in a fight, but the social warfare takes a toll on me.

It feels like everyone I encounter has some sort of problem with me. I wouldn't be surprised if the workers at the pizza place mess around with my food. I've had some verbal confrontations with some of the employees there. Now all I can think of when we order pizza is what they did to tamper with my meal. People close to me seem to think that I'm just paranoid, but they don't see the stuff that I see. I don't know if it's all in my head, but I'm scared to look up in case I see someone giving me a weird look. I'm already anxious just knowing that they are, so I guess it'd be no different if I just looked up.

The days seem to get slower with each passing shift. The shift could almost be finished, but I'll feel like I've been here for a week. Even with all the machinery roaring around me, I can still hear the clock mocking me as it slowly ticks, each passing second forcing me to count along with it. The end of the day never creeps up on me. I count down the final minute and breathe a small sigh of relief as I make it through another day. The sigh of relief is short lived as I come to the painful realization that I get to do this all over again tomorrow.

Everyone shares the locker room in the back, so it gets pretty packed back there after the shift is over. I move quickly and keep to myself as I gather my belongings and get changed into the jeans and t-shirt I arrived in this morning. The atmosphere is what you'd expect from a factory setting: loud, obnoxious and crude. A decade ago, I may have fit in better with these men. Times do change.

I head for the exit, and I overhear a couple guys talking. It appears they're looking in my direction as they converse. What's their problem? I don't even talk to those guys, so who are they to talk about me? Once upon a time, I would have built up the courage to confront them about it. Nowadays, I hold back in order to avoid putting myself in a dangerous situation. If I confront them in front of all the workers in the locker room, I'm just painting a giant, red target on my back. In this environment, you never know how things could escalate. I escape into my shell, pull my hood over my head and exit through the back door.

My car engine purrs loudly as I turn the key in the ignition. I wish it was louder in order to drown out the thoughts I'm tossing around. I swear I heard one of the guys say my name and one of the other guys say something about a liar as I was passing by. I can't help but analyze this. These guys can be rough around the edges. All it would take is for someone to have it out for me, start a rumor and get some of the men in there riled up. Who wouldn't want to tell their friends they beat the snot out of a former Olympic boxer?

Should I tell somebody about what I'm thinking and how I'm feeling? Part of me knows I'm completely overthinking these situations, but like I said before, if you tell yourself certain things long enough, eventually you'll begin to believe them. The notch on the radio gets twisted heavily to the right as I try to drown out my feelings, at least until I get home. "Sweet Caroline" blasts through the speakers as I speed down the city streets, trying to outrun my thoughts.

Although it's been a rough few years, it's nice to know I can call Steve and get his trusted opinion on things. We've gone through similar life experiences, and he can always talk me down off the mental cliff I've created in my mind. I'm going to need that tonight. I feel like I'm always bothering him with my problems, but I don't know who else to turn to. He always reminds me that I can talk to him about anything, but I just feel bad sometimes, stressing him out with my problems. It's embarrassing, the way I feel every day. Every time we talk, I have a new group of individuals who are coming after me or threatening me. He must think I'm losing my mind.

All the lights are off as I enter my dark, empty home. My son, Tanner, has a hockey tournament in Barrie this weekend, so I knew they would be gone by the time I got back. My wife, Franny, took him and our daughter, Victoria, so I have the house to myself for the rest of the weekend. After emotionally draining days like this, I always look forward to leaning on my family for some support, so I wish they were here tonight. I leave the lights off as I walk through the hallway toward the phone. I dial my brother's home number, but I hang up before it starts ringing. I don't know why, but it just doesn't seem like a good time to talk right now. Besides, I remember calling him a couple days ago with a very similar scenario. Maybe I can deal with this one on my own tonight. Steve has talked me through enough stuff this week.

I head into the kitchen and discover a note on the dining room table from Fran:

Jamie,

I cooked up a lasagna and put a couple pieces for you on a plate to microwave. Hope you have a good weekend. Don't miss us too much. Love you.

P.S. your mother stopped by with some boxes she found in storage with yours and Steve's boxing stuff. They're in the basement xo

My skin curled as I read the last part of that note. I haven't looked through any of that stuff since the Olympics all those years ago. *Why would I?* Unless they have a time machine in there, I'm not interested. I heat up my lasagna.

The thought of going back to work tomorrow feeds my anxiety. As the night gets darker, my mind begins to wander farther away from stability. Any bit of composure I struggled to hold onto during the day dissipates, and I decide I'll pour myself a drink to help ease my troubled mind. I head downstairs to my bar to fix myself a quick whiskey before bed. Maybe a couple quick whiskeys; we'll see how it goes. The first couple gulps swim down my throat effortlessly.

As hard as I try to ignore them, I can see the boxes Fran mentioned stacked neatly in the middle of the floor by the couches. I forgot how much stuff my father had archived for Steve and I. Those boxes represent my past. Since I can't change the past, there's no reason to hash up my boxing career all over again. Part of me just wants to grab my boxes and throw them to the curb. Boxing gave me everything, and then took it all away. I have no interest in going down memory lane; I do that enough on my own.

As I stare at the boxes across the room, I finish off my first glass of whiskey and pour myself a second. I can't help but be tempted to just take a quick look. *Screw it.* I sit down on the couch, but I hesitate to open a box. It's not like there are any surprises in here. It's my life as I've lived it. It's just that, even though there were so many incredible memories, the painful ones are so strong and lingering that it's tough for me to talk about boxing without bringing up the elephant in the room.

I push my boxes aside and pull Steve's closer. Maybe I'll dive into his boxes instead. My big brother had so many amazing highlights to his career. I open up the box and pull out a couple photo albums. There are so many newspaper articles detailing his fights.

"Steve Pagendam of the St. Catharines Boxing Club earned

a unanimous decision over Canadian champion Rick Ranelli"

"Steve Pagendam, billed as the premier lightweight in the

St. Catharines Boxing Club, showed his stuff in the main event

Friday night"

"PAGENDAM SCORES KO.

Steve Pagendam, who usually uses his classy style to out

point his opponents, proved he can go the other route when he has

to"

I always loved watching Steve fight. I'm in awe looking through

the pictures in this photo album. Try to picture the legendary

George Foreman, Joe Frazier and Muhammad Ali black-and-white

photos; that's what Steve's photos remind me of. There are

beautiful pictures of Steve in the ring with his long hair coming

through the top of his headpiece, looking so focused on his

opponent. There are a few pages of pictures of him in Finland with

the Canadian national team standing outside, proudly representing

our country. Every photo captures a different side of him: the

competitor, Mr. Smooth, Wham Bam Pagendam.

As I flip through his photo album with a smile across my

face, I keep seeing my boxes in my peripherals. It's one thing to look through Steve's stuff and reminisce; it's another whole thing with mine. I pack Steve's box back up and put it aside. I decide that's enough for the night. I pick up my box and make my way to the closet to store it away with all the other crap I don't want to look at.

In picking up the box, I noticed something sticking out of the top. I put the box down on the couch and pull at it. It's a picture of Steve and I sparring against each other at the St. Catharines Boxing Club. We look like we're having the time of our lives. Our coach, Hank Boone, is in the corner laughing, but also yelling at us to keep our hands up and keep moving. Those were very enjoyable times for me. I was probably only fifteen at the time.

My interest is slightly piqued. I lowered my guard a bit. What else is in this box? I pull out another album. I can't believe there's a picture of me from when I fought John John Molina. It isn't the best quality picture, but it has a lot of meaning to me.

A large printed photo of me and my father, Les, sits on the very first page of the album. It's from Darren Tucker's fundraiser, the event that put me on a new course in life. There are multiple articles in here about my Olympic medal aspirations.

"I'll bring home a medal – Pagendam"

"Boxer has sights on Olympic gold"

"At the summer Olympics, the goal is gold"

The box is filled with years' and years' worth of articles our parents must have kept for us. Wow, some of these fights I don't even remember. As I read through the hours' worth of news clippings, I get to the back pages and see an article from October 1989. The headline reads "Olympics still haunt Pagendam." I slam the book shut, spilling some of my whiskey on the coffee table in the process.

I put my head in my palms and try my hardest to repel the negative thoughts that are attempting to flood into my brain. As I pull my hands away from my face, I see there is one item left in my box. I take a big breath in and pull out a tape that reads *1988 Olympics - Jamie Pagendam*. How can something that happened almost three decades ago still be defining me? Why am I scared to watch this again?

I would love nothing more than to be able to sit with my family and friends and recall all the great times boxing gave me. I want to be able to have my grandkids sit on my lap as I tell them how their grandpa used to travel to different parts of the world and fight boxers from different countries. Tell them that although I've had some very tough times, I've learned from them, and I became stronger and wiser because of it.

I have so many stories I could share, but I want to share them with pride and joy in my heart. That's why I need to get past this mental block. I need to face this traumatic moment head on and put it to rest. The whiskey in my right hand quickly finds the back of my throat. The tape in my left hand is removed from its casing. Tonight, I go back to the 1988 Olympics.

CHAPTER II

Go Your Own Way

1977

Jamie Pagendam

The competitiveness I had, even at a young age, was so fierce that it was no wonder I excelled at sports. I was emotionally invested in anything that involved a definitive winner being named. The competitive spirit I've had throughout my life could easily be attributed to the fact I was always the smallest kid in my class, on the sports team; I was overlooked. Some of it was due to the fact that I'm the youngest of my two brothers, Steve and Jeff, but with that came my obsession with wanting to prove myself.

Steve is five years older than I am, so I got to watch him compete in all kinds of different sports when I was really young. Eventually, I got into hockey and football as well, but hockey was the sport where I shone the brightest. I hated to lose, so I did everything I could to score and make sure my team came out on top. One time, I refused to come off the ice for a line change because we were down by a goal. The coach waited until I skated by the bench, reached over the boards and literally lifted me off the ice. I was around ten years old at the time, so it wouldn't have taken much to lift me over the boards. What can I say? I didn't want to leave the ice until I was able to get my team in a position to win.

I knew Steve was getting into boxing, but I didn't know all that much about the sport. I knew the general concept was based around punching an opponent, and I had seen highlights of it on the sports channels, but I wasn't too sure what it was all about. I asked my dad, Les, if I could watch Steve fight in his first match at Bill Burgoyne Arena in St. Catharines. This would be my first taste of live boxing. It was a new, exciting experience for me.

It was definitely a different environment than the ones I had been introduced to before. It wasn't long before I learned how rowdy boxing fans could get. During the fights, the crowd was constantly yelling, screaming and swearing. As an eleven-year-old boy, I enjoyed the energy and the electricity in the air. The crowd "ooh"ing and "aw"ing. The audience grasping the edges of their seats in anticipation of the next big moment.

I was jealous that Steve got to take part in this. Watching him compete in his fight, even though he ended up losing and breaking his nose, inspired me in such a way that compelled me to want to try my hand at this boxing thing.

I sat in the back of the car as we drove my brother to the hospital, bleeding profusely from his broken nose. Buckled in beside me was a pretty big trophy that he received for participating in the fight, even though he lost. So you can get your butt handed to you and still go home with some hardware to show for it? Sounds good to me.

None of the kids at my school had ever boxed before. I thought, *I could be doing something that none of them have ever even thought about doing, and they'd have to respect me for that.* Being picked on and bullied a lot was something I didn't like having to deal with in my childhood. Even though I was feisty, I didn't know the proper way to respond to someone picking on me. I didn't know what to say, how to react or how to defend myself. I knew if I excelled in boxing and people heard about how well I was doing, I would gain their respect. And if they still wanted to pick on me after that, then, I guessed I'd just have to pop them in the mouth.

This newly found desire to box didn't resonate with my dad. I brought it up in the car that night, and he shut it down straight away. His argument was that I was only eleven years old and too small to be competing in this type of combat sport. At that time, I was only sixty pounds soaking wet, and that's being generous.

He also figured Steve was done boxing after breaking his nose, but that wasn't the case either. You know if you break your nose in your first fight, and you're back in the gym the very next week, you really want to succeed in the sport. So if a broken nose wasn't going to stop Steve, then my dad saying no wasn't going to stop me either.

I spent the next few weeks harassing him at every turn, trying to convince him to let me go to the club with Steve. It got to the point where any time I was in the same room as my dad, we would be arguing about the prospects of me boxing. I would get so frustrated during these exchanges that I would throw a tantrum, tears pouring down my beet-red face as I screamed at the top of my lungs. It wasn't just my dad. My mother didn't understand why we would want to join a violent sport like this either. It was Steve who was able to convince our parents to let me try it out. He said to them, "Let Jamie give it shot. We'll see how much he likes it after he takes some punches to the head. He might not like the feeling of getting banged around too much." After that, I got my dad's blessing, and I was ready to prove a couple shots to the head weren't going to slow me down.

The Port Dalhousie Boxing Club, 1977

It was called the Port Dalhousie Boxing Club, and this is where my boxing journey began. The club was owned and operated by former Irish Champion Jimmy Neil. Steve had already been training there for a couple months, so he knew everyone. He introduced me to Jimmy, and then we got right into training. There was no messing around. If you came to train, then you were all business once you put your workout gear on. The environment was even more interesting than the arena I had watched the fights in. I was witnessing firsthand the blood, sweat and tears that went into becoming a fighter. It was very intense, and you could feel the competitive energy in the air.

Everyone was always willing to share tips and help each other get better, but at the same time you were there to get yourself to new levels individually. The technical aspects came naturally to me. So naturally, in fact, that Jimmy felt confident to schedule me my first fight six weeks after I had joined the club. Whenever we got to work closely with Jimmy, he was always a good teacher. He wholeheartedly believed the best way to learn was by experiencing real ring action. Some would say it was like throwing us to the wolves, but you can't become a lion unless you've wrestled your fair share of wolves.

I was feeling good about stepping into the ring. The guys who trained at the club were all pumping me up during the weeks leading up to it. I wouldn't say I was ready, but I was optimistic, and I thought it'd be a fun experience. As a kid, all the pent-up energy inside of me was ready to burst. I didn't really know what to expect. All I knew was when the bell rang, I was going to go out there and throw as many punches as I could, and I wasn't going to stop throwing until they told me to.

Jimmy matched me up with a fighter named Rip Rod Montgomery during one of their annual summer boxing events. They would hold two or three boxing shows like this every summer at a really nice outdoor venue called the Lacrosse Bowl in Port Dalhousie. All the guys from the club were there, whether they were competing on the card or just there to support the guys fighting. I felt motivated to put on a great show for them. I definitely looked the part, rocking my brand-new white boxing shoes that my parents had bought for me.

The bell rang and I did exactly what I wanted to do: started throwing punches in bunches. I backed Rip Rod into the corner and just started whaling away on him, not yet knowing too much about proper technique or anything like that. It felt like I was just swinging and trying to land as much as possible. I ended up beating on him so good in the first round that he didn't even want to come out for the second, so the referee stopped the fight.

Even though I remember my first fight being nothing more than a choppy, one-sided slugfest, Steve told me it looked like I had been boxing for twenty years in there. Jimmy Neil was even puffing his chest out after the match saying that I reminded him of a younger version of himself. Those were massive compliments from two people I looked up to a lot. I was all teeth as I stood in the center of the ring with the referee, hand raised high.

All the fighters from the club were patting me on the back as I hauled around my trophy and my complimentary hot dog. I was on Cloud 9. I felt like I was the second coming of Muhammad Ali. I ran around for the rest of the event, watching and cheering on the other fighters as they competed. I was in Heaven, and I figured it could only get better from here.

It was obvious to anyone walking through the gym that I was by far the youngest fighter at the club. Everyone else who worked out at the gym was in their teens or older. It was important for me, being that age, to have Steve at the club. I knew he wouldn't let anyone take advantage of me or try to punk me. The other fighters in the club never made me feel like an outsider though. Despite the age gap, I always felt like one of the boys.

A fighter by the name of Dave Morris was someone who really took a liking to me. As an eleven-year-old, I felt so cool that an eighteen-year-old young man had taken me under his wing and wanted to spend time with me, help me get better and joke around with me. I got him to show me how to do the Ali Shuffle but I wasn't as good at it as he was.

Dave was someone I watched closely during our workouts and tried to mimic his movements. I remember how smooth he was on his feet, in both his training and during his fights. He had style and swagger when he walked around the room, and it was contagious. There was a cockiness about him that I kind of took on myself as I got to be a more established fighter. Not cocky in a bad way or an arrogant way. It was more like a self-confidence, mixed with some boldness and a cheeky personality. I believed in myself and wanted everybody to know that.

Dave was the top dog at the club and Jimmy's golden boy. He got a lot of the attention from the coaches, especially Jimmy, because they saw him as the club's best fighter. They were grooming and molding him to become a champion one day. Everyone knew that Dave had loads of potential to go far in this sport. I was always super excited to watch his fights. It's strange, but Dave Morris never won a Provincial or National Championship during his boxing career. He was truly an amazing fighter, but he was in a very tough and competitive weight division. He definitely had all the capabilities to succeed at any level of boxing he wanted. I really appreciated him as a friend and a role model during the beginning stages of my boxing career. More than anything though, I wanted to impress my older brother by being able to fit in with this group. It didn't take me long at all to feel comfortable in this environment.

The second fight I ever had was against Vernon McGriff from Buffalo, who ended up becoming my first ever "rival." Still riding the high from my win a few weeks prior, I had all the confidence in the world that I was going to be able to dominate like I did against Rip Rod. Jimmy matched me up with McGriff despite the fact that he had way more experience than me, to the tune of twenty-five to thirty fights. For such a young kid, he was already a seasoned fighter. I thought I might do okay considering how I did in my first match, and clearly Jimmy thought I would match up well against him. This was not the case at all.

I could not land a single punch during the match. Well, maybe that's an exaggeration, but not too far off from the truth either. The punches I threw were finding nothing but air as I tried to hit him with every kind of move possible. I grew so frustrated in the ring that I began to literally cry out of anger during the match. That's something you don't see every day. The harder I attempted to throw my punches, the more horribly I missed, and the faster the tears streamed down my cheeks and dripped to the canvas.

Vernon and I would go on to have at least ten fights spanning over four years. Every time we fought, I would learn something new from him. We embraced our friendly rivalry, trying to one up each other every time we fought. I don't know who ended up getting the final upper hand, but we built a lasting comradery through our shared experience with each other. We ended up becoming quite good friends during this time and, oddly enough, on a couple occasions we would ride up to a boxing event together, share a hotel room, and then the next day we would fight each other at the event. Vernon later went on to become the U.S. National Champion.

1978

Jimmy was occasionally getting me fights as I continued to dedicate myself to learning the craft. I was still the newest guy at the club until a fighter named Bill Hardy walked into the gym with his uncle, Hank Boone. Just by looking at Billy, you could tell he had decent boxing potential due to his athletic frame. While Billy was talking to some of the trainers, I noticed this Hank guy was walking around the club, checking out all the equipment and examining some of the fighters while they worked out.

As weeks went by, Hank would often stick around the gym after dropping off Billy and just observe from the back of the club. He would sometimes give us some encouragement if we happened to walk by him. Nothing too crazy, just a quick "nice work out there" or "keep it up." Hank was in his thirties, looked to be in pretty good shape, and he had this aura about himself. You could always feel his presence when he was at the gym.

It wasn't long before Hank started building up some rapport with Jimmy and the other trainers by jumping into conversations between and after our training sessions. Before we knew it, he started helping out around the club by wrapping up fighter's hands, putting on gloves, holding up hand pads and any other way he could get himself involved. Once he was in this position to be around the fighters, along with the trust he was gaining among many trainers at the club, Hank became a mainstay.

There were a lot of talented fighters at Port Dalhousie Boxing Club while I was there. Everyone was willing to put in the work, soak up information like a sponge and try to make progress every day. Since Dave Morris was the top prospect at our club, he received most of the coaches' attention. It made sense strictly because Provincials were coming up soon, along with many other important events. However, it alienated the other fighters who had similar goals but maybe weren't held in as high regard.

Unfortunately, in boxing gyms, this happens quite a bit. It happens in most sports, quite frankly. All it takes is for the coach to see a special talent in one of the players, and often that will be followed up with some favoritism. I mean, at the time, I was only eleven or twelve, so it's understandable that they didn't invest as much time into my training.

While everyone was dedicated to making sure Dave had all the resources he needed, Hank was making sure Steve and I were getting the attention he believed we deserved. Hank had never boxed before, or even coached boxing for that matter, but he loved the sport so much, and you could tell. The way Hank spoke to us made us feel like our talents were appreciated. While he held up the hand pads for Steve and I, he would tell us we were going to be champions. "You boys are going places."

It was after a tournament that Jimmy couldn't attend that Hank really started setting in motion a plan to take us out of the Port Dalhousie Boxing Club. Hank worked Steve's corner when he won the silver medal at the tournament, losing to the very well-respected Sean O'Sullivan in the finals. That weekend must have given Hank the idea, or the confidence he needed, to try and start his own club.

He made it clear to us that he didn't think we were going to get the proper training we needed at Port Dalhousie. At this point it made sense to roll with Hank and leave the club. Nothing against Jimmy; he had a smart boxing IQ and was a good coach, but he never showed a belief in us becoming anything in boxing the way Hank did.

The idea was that Hank was going to find us a place to train. He promised he was going to find us fights, coach us and that the gym would be built around the Pagendam brothers. I liked the sound of that, especially coming from Hank's golden tongue. You have to ask yourself this question: Why would two brothers who started at the club in Port Dalhousie leave that club and go with someone completely unknown in boxing? Because, as much as Hank made us believe in ourselves, we, in turn, began believing in Hank.

Hank talked to our dad and laid out his plan of action for us. It's one thing to be boxing out of an established gym with trusted trainers from the community; it's another to join a brand new club run by a guy who has no previous boxing credentials and who we've realistically only known for a couple months. Our dad gave us the go ahead, and so began our journey with Hank Boone.

At the start, it was just going to be Steve, Billy and I, but the gym Hank had found for us was going to be shared with a kick boxing club. We don't know how he managed to have ins like this, but he did, and he sniffed this place out. The club was called Jocelyn's Karate School, and it was run by brothers Rocky and Jessie Zolnerchuck. These guys were tough as nails, and we were able to pick up some great techniques from them during our stint at this club.

We were only planning on working out there temporarily until Hank was able to lock down a place for us to train permanently. The best part about training out of this gym was the amount of sparring we were able to mix in. All the kick boxers were always willing to compete in a few rounds. Just like at Jimmy's club, I was by far the youngest fighter at the gym. Anytime I sparred, it was with men who were much stronger and bigger than I was. They would have to take it easier on me, but even through that, I was able to learn many things and grow as a fighter. They would let me whale away on them while they moved around the ring trying to simulate a fight as best they could against an eleven-year-old. It was probably hilarious to watch this tiny child trying to compete against fully grown men. Steve and I, whether it was sparring or an actual fight, always gave our opponents fits with our southpaw stances. We both had a big left hand.

Spring 1979

The most drastic change I noticed being at the new club was that Steve and I were getting all the attention, and I loved it. Hank liked it like that. He brought in other trainers to help out, and once he felt comfortable with the situation, he pulled the trigger on a property that would ultimately become the St. Catharines Boxing Club.

The layout of the club was very unique in comparison to your average, more traditional club. For starters, the property was a bungalow across from a factory in a poverty-stricken neighborhood. The house wasn't even renovated to look more like a gym. The living room, which was the biggest area of the property, was where Hank built the boxing ring. The heavy bags were hanging from the bedroom ceilings. There were areas of the house dedicated to shadow boxing, skipping and other low-maintenance activities with mirrors set up along the walls.

We would shower downstairs in the basement, which was also home to a few speed bags. It was definitely different, but we enjoyed it. It was such a dark, grungy place, but it reminded us of something Rocky Balboa would have trained out of early on in his career. Our sweat, tears and blood flowed as we made history out of this little shack of a gym. The foundation of our boxing careers were built within the brick walls of this house.

I was serious about boxing, but I didn't want to stop playing hockey either. I was on the Bantam All-Star Team in Merritton, and this was destined to be our best season yet. We were favorites to take home the OMHA championship. The coach for this team knew I was boxing and knew what this season meant for the hockey club, so he made the assistant coach cut me from the roster.

Even though I was boxing, it rarely ever conflicted with any of my other sports, so I had a hard time understanding why I had been cut from the team. After some convincing from the other staff members, the head coach decided to let me play on the team. However, it was not a healthy relationship by any means.

After our first exhibition game, the coach charged into the change room and locked onto me like I was his target. I don't know why he had such a big problem with me boxing, but he was not afraid to voice his opinion on the matter. He said I had to choose boxing or hockey. I loved both sports so much, so it was too difficult to just choose one. Since I couldn't decide, the coach gave me an ultimatum. If I missed any hockey-related activities due to boxing, I would be suspended for a certain amount of games. Training for boxing usually took place during the evenings, while hockey was early in the morning, so I didn't think it would ever become an issue.

Deeper into the season, I finally found myself in a situation where the two sports conflicted with one another. I had a hockey practice on the same night as one of my fights. I felt a fight was much more important than one hockey practice, so of course I went to the fight. My punishment was that I would miss the first playoff game when we returned home from a tournament in Philadelphia. I was determined to outperform everybody at this tournament and win the MVP trophy so the coach would see that I could both box and play hockey without it hurting my on-ice performance.

As I set my goal, I would go on to accomplish winning the tournament's MVP honors. I played my heart out. It felt like I was scoring on every single shift. This made me feel great about my current situation. I was still excelling at hockey, while also being able to dedicate the time I needed to sharpen my boxing skills. There were no doubts in my mind that I could excel at hockey while pursuing boxing. It's funny to think that nowadays boxing is a widely used form of off-ice training for professional and amateur hockey players. Athletes from all types of different sports partake in boxing as a training method. I guess I was just ahead of my time.

My celebration didn't last too long, however. When I was walking back to where the team was staying, I came across some teammates talking. I overheard them say some nasty things about me. Among the comments were things like:

"Jamie didn't deserve to win the MVP award this

weekend."

"He's clearly not as dedicated as we are to this sport."

"He should just give up hockey and stick to boxing."

I took a deep breath in, and when I had exhaled I knew that was going to be my last year playing hockey. I was never trying to be a bad teammate; I just liked to prove myself. I tried my best to fit in and help the team win, but there's always jealousy and there will always be politics. I finished out the rest of the season, and that was it for me.

Sometimes it only takes a couple moments like this to take away the love you have for something. I still had fond memories of my time playing hockey, but after this, my desire to play was seriously fading. On the flip side, I had more time to dedicate to boxing now. With other distractions no longer an issue, it was clear now that my ultimate goal was to eventually make the Olympic boxing team.

CHAPTER III

Remember the Name

1980–1981

One thing I had was killer instinct. If I had a guy hurt, I finished him because I loved to finish off fighters. I didn't want to just beat him; I wanted to humiliate the guy opposite me. That was my mindset in everything I did. When I was playing hockey, if we were winning by five, I wanted to be winning by seven. Even later in life, when I was coaching minor hockey, I didn't want my team to ever take their foot off the gas pedal. Maybe I should have gone a little easier on them; they were only twelve after all. But I wanted them to be as hungry and competitive as I was. In everything I did, I wanted to leave a lasting impact.

I knew how I wanted my story to play out: I wanted to be seen as a master of the craft, who racked up win after win in dominating fashion. The end of my story would have me standing tall in victory after conquering the entirety of my foes. Hank was on the exact same page as me. He saw the picture I wanted to paint, so he provided me the canvas.

There was a time when Steve had taken some time away from boxing to work on a new chapter in his life, and I didn't see him at the club very often. Even through that, I stuck with boxing and continued to love it. I had no reservations about going to the gym without Steve because I was becoming very comfortable being around Hank and some of the other fighters at the club. There was a real trust being built within the walls of the St. Catharines Boxing Club.

Since Hank had never boxed before, he didn't always have the answers when it came to specific technical things. But at least he was smart enough to realize this and was willing to bring in coaches who could help the fighters learn new styles and techniques. Rufus Johnson was well immersed in the surrounding amateur boxing circuit. He was involved in building up the New York scene, just over the border from us. Hank was able to connect with him, which led to us getting fights and sparring in the States.

Hank would always network with the different coaches when we would travel around to fight shows. Rufus and Hank seemed to like each other, which led to some good collaborative training sessions with the American fighters. I got to train with Rufus on and off for about a year. He would come over from New York to our club every couple weeks.

Rufus was a good technical coach and was instrumental in helping me become a better rounded fighter. He was the one who taught me the proper way to distribute my weight in order to get the most power behind my punches. I have to give him credit for defining my uppercut and my lethal right hook, because that's basically what we focused on when I had the chance to work with him. We never worked on the basic stuff, like jabbing. He was more focused on teaching me the under and over combinations. Those punches ended up being my bread and butter throughout my entire boxing career.

Rufus was easy to learn from because he was so calm. He wasn't a hype man. He didn't make it about himself; it was about me. You know, sometimes when people work the hand pads, they're looking around to see who's watching them. It's almost as if they want an audience. Rufus wasn't about that. He would take me aside, away from everyone else at the club, and we would work on the same techniques over and over again until it was engrained in the fibers of my fists. He didn't want me being distracted by the eyeballs; he wanted me to be laser-focused on myself. Working with Rufus definitely built up my confidence to new levels. I could tell he really enjoyed coming down to visit our club.

Most clubs can't afford to let their fighters train for free, but never once did Hank ask us to pay a dime. It was all out of his pocket. All of our traveling and training was covered. All we had to do was show up and work hard, and he was happy. I guess you could say we indirectly helped keep the club afloat by headlining the monthly fight shows Hank would set up at the Canadian Automotive Workers hall in St. Catharines. Since Steve and I were

35

such popular names on the local boxing circuit, we were always able to draw huge crowds to the events.

Hank would set everything up and promote the event around the Pagendam boys. Steve would often be the main event because he was older and in a higher weight class than me. I was just content to be one of the main reasons people were coming out to watch. I felt like a minor celebrity. Based on the number of people who would attend, it's probably safe to say the club was doing well financially.

Hank kept on hustling and started hosting local bingo nights with his wife Sherri to raise money for the club. All these things were done to make sure we were taken care of. It was a team effort, and it was heartening to see how dedicated our coach was to helping build up the St. Catharines Boxing Club. He did all of this while simultaneously working a full-time job at General Motors. It felt like his life revolved around boxing just as much as ours did.

I would hear the honk from Hank's sports car early in the morning as he waited outside my house. He was gracious enough to drive me back and forth to the boxing club. When I got old enough, he would be waiting outside my house, leaning up against the car's passenger door, and he would toss me the keys. How many kids that age can say they got to drive a black Camaro Z-28 down the street? I would think to myself, *This is what it's going to be like when I make it to the pros.* I would sit at home and think about stuff like that. Turning pro with Hank in my corner, driving sports cars, living in a big house—these were the dreams I had, and Hank was giving me a glimpse into that lifestyle.

Hank was always an invested coach, but as time went on I began seeing him as more than just my coach and began seeing him as my mentor and a friend. I could feel how important I was to him, and it was nice to feel this type of appreciation from someone I looked up to.

Eventually, I began finding myself at Hank's house a lot. His son Brody was a little younger than me, so I was kind of like a playmate for him. Hank would take his wife out for dinner or a show, and I would watch over Brody and hang out with him. Hank would also give me little jobs to do around the house, like mow his lawn or wash his car, so I could make a little petty cash for myself. It got to the point where I was pretty much there every weekend, and occasionally I'd stop in on weeknights too.

The Boone family treated me like I was one of their own. They had all the things a teenager desired, and they unselfishly let me use it all. I could take a dip in their swimming pool whenever I wanted. Hank would take me out on his motorcycle. At times, he would let me sit at the front of the bike, and I could help him steer it around corners. They had ATVs to wheel around on during the warm months and snowmobiles during the winter months. To me, it felt like an amusement park every time I went over there. I never had anything like this at my disposal before. We just didn't grow up with these types of luxuries around my house.

During this time, my family would go days without seeing me because I would just stay over at Hank's for the entire weekend. The amount of time I was spending there was a growing concern for my parents. They thought I was being negatively influenced by the Boones, and it wasn't lining up with our family values. I thought it was ridiculous that they were even bringing this up as an issue. I was a teenager; I was just enjoying myself.

They thought Hank had too much control over the way I was dictating my life. I was training with him, hanging out with him and practically living with him. My dad had many talks with me about it, but I didn't understand where he was coming from. It was in one ear and out the other. I was having so much fun over there, especially compared to being at home, that I just thought my parents were being jealous.

I remember a specific day where my dad was going to drive me to the airport, and Hank came over to see me off. Hank usually drove me to the airport, but my dad insisted he would take me this time around. Right before we left, Hank said to my dad, "You take care of my son there." That comment set my dad off. He snapped back aggressively at him and said, "Hey, this is my son, not yours!" I'll never forget that because it felt like a very weird situation. I was confused. It felt awkward. I'd never seen two adults bark at each other like that, especially when it involved me. I really saw my dad in a different light after that, and it was in a negative way.

These moments put a strain on my relationship with my dad. From my point of view, it appeared as if my dad was trying to put a wedge between Hank and I for his own selfish benefit. That made me want to be at home even less. The inside of my house was foggy with a thick cloud of tension. An awkward wall was being built up between us. It was around this time I made the decision to stop going to church with my family. My dad was very involved in the church, so I know it bothered him that I didn't show much interest in that path. The Boones weren't churchgoers; many of the people I trained with weren't Christians, so I started to slowly separate myself from the church. I think I still believed in God, but I wanted to do my own thing. I was sick of being restrained by rules.

These little moments never changed my relationship with Hank. He put me on a pedestal and made me feel invincible. Nothing was impossible for me when I was with him. With my dad, there were so many laws to follow, unnecessary lectures and guilt trips. As a teenager, I naturally gravitated toward Hank because it better suited the lifestyle I wanted to live. I felt free with Hank. He was promising me the world, and I felt destined to get to that promised land.

The Fortuna Challenge, 1982

As I got a little older, everything started moving really fast for me. Hank was getting me fights twice, sometimes three times a week.

The wins were racking up, and I had already accomplished more than some boxers had in their entire career. At age sixteen, I had over 130 amateur fights and was building up quite the resume for myself. I had gained such notoriety among the boxing community that I received the great honor of being inducted into the St. Catharines Boxing Hall of Fame. So far, my story was playing out exactly how I had imagined.

Although it wasn't mentioned often enough, many heralded Hank Boone as one of the top matchmakers in the sport. Tony Unitas, a well-known trainer in Canada, was noted saying that he believed Hank was "the best matchmaker in boxing." He was a good coach, but he was a master matchmaker and fight promoter. His ability to build up and promote fights was unmatched by no other in Canada. Russ Anber, a well-respected boxing analyst, publicly stated that Boone was the best southpaw coach in Canada and maybe even North America. Since he was my coach and mentor, I was the one who got to reap the benefits of his talents the most, along with Steve. A lot of people didn't like Hank's style because he didn't play the political game, but he had a way he liked to operate, and he never steered away from that. He always had his fingers on the pulse of the surrounding boxing circuits.

He would go out and watch local fight shows from time to time. There was this one night that a young man named Rob Fortuna wowed the crowd and caught his eye. Hank witnessed Rob take home the Intermediate Canadian Championship, which was the division I would be able to join when I eventually turned seventeen.

What Hank did that night, and for weeks after, solidified his spot as the boldest matchmaker at the time. He went around the event boasting that I could beat Rob, hands down. He was telling anyone who would listen. At first, no one put much weight into what Hank was saying, but the more he said it, the more people wanted to see it. "My boy, my fighter Jamie Pagendam would walk right through Fortuna." This is the type of brass and cockiness that rubbed people the wrong way, but lo and behold, he got the fight set up because of it.

Hank was always great at putting us in the ring with fighters who would be even match-ups for us. Many times he would try and put us in there with fighters who were a tiny bit more experienced which, over time, made us sharper fighters. But this fight against Rob would be putting me in a fight against the best fighter in the intermediate division. Like I said, as I got older, everything started moving faster. If Hank thought I was ready to make that kind of leap, I was ready to back up what he was saying.

He definitely knew how to unleash the beast from within Steve and I. He did whatever it took to motivate us to want to bull through our opponent in that ring. He would tell us things that the opposing fighter or their coaches had said about us, none of it true. We would believe it, though, and it made us want to get into the ring and rip the guy's head off his shoulders. I loved the whole situation with Rob, because it was a pivotal moment in my career. Win or lose, this match was going to turn me from the boy into the man.

Even as the fight got closer, Hank was still boasting to everyone around the city that Rob did not know what he was in for. These were strong words coming from the underdog's camp. Rob was growing into a young man with broad shoulders and a mature body frame. Meanwhile, I was still very small for my age, even at sixteen.

As much as Hank was boosting my ego, this match was just as important to him. He had his agenda. Whenever I would win a fight, it only built up the resume of my coach, my trainer and my handler, Hank. Rob Fortuna came from the Niagara Falls boxing scene. There's a boxing stable there that has been around a lot longer than Hank, and he was always rubbing shoulders with these guys. Hank would brag about the kind of talent he was working with at the club, so if I were to beat Rob Fortuna, I was not only upping my game, but I was validating Hank's boxing acumen.

Hank boasting and bragging about how we could take on any fighter, any day, created some animosity between our club and the other surrounding clubs. It definitely rubbed off on us. Even though that wasn't our personalities per se, just by association, we appeared to be that way too. Hank definitely wasn't well liked among the boxing community. He was a likeable guy, but you had to be on his side to see that. Many weren't.

The target on our backs made me train harder. You don't see many teenagers train the way I trained. I didn't do a lot of road work at that point in my career, but I spent many hours in the gym hitting the bag, hitting the pads, sparring; I was well prepared. I always trained my buns off, but I had something important to prove this time around. Beating Fortuna would propel me leaps and bounds ahead of where I currently sat in my progression. If I could secure this victory, it would catapult me into a position where I could fast-track my career to where I wanted it.

The Fortuna Fights, 1982

The way I boxed Rob in the first match was smart. He planted himself in the middle of the ring and was looking to trade. I knew I could pick him apart in his flat-footed stance by dancing around him, staying light on my feet and consistently landing my jab. This was my game plan for the much-bigger Fortuna, and it worked wonders. Although Rob dropped me in the second round for a knockdown, I managed to score enough points in the other rounds to collect a unanimous decision victory!

However, Fortuna's camp was attempting to taint my victory: "Jamie only won because he was dancing around so much." "Jamie isn't strong enough to stand and trade with Rob so he has to run around the ring." "If Jamie and Rob stood in the center and traded, he would get knocked out." The talk bothered me. I had won the fight. I told Hank to set up a rematch.

There I go again. That's my mindset. You tell me I can't do something, and I'll prove you wrong. I felt disrespected. My mindset going into that fight was, okay, I won't dance around, I'll stand flat-footed with him. Every time he comes in, I'm going to smash him. I wanted to beat him so bad that he would never be the same fighter again. This was going to be my division now. There would be no doubt in anyone's mind who the real champ was after this fight.

The second fight with Rob was a master class of power punching. If anybody had any questions about my power, they were answered during the bout with Fortuna. I was often seen as a smooth, quick fighter, but now people had to be very aware of the knockout power I possessed.

I stood right where Rob's coaches wanted me to, and I began landing punishing shots on their fighter. I popped him countless times, leading to multiple standing eight counts. I planted myself in the center of the ring, I did not dance and I achieved the same result. Except this time, I didn't just secure the victory, I made an impact. Everybody would know the name Jamie Pagendam after the way I won that fight. Fortuna tasted leather for three straight rounds, but to his credit he never backed down and was able to go the distance with me.

Steve told me after the fight that he couldn't believe how swollen Fortuna's cheekbones got throughout the match. I took pride in the fact that I was able to inflict that much damage on a quality opponent. Once again, I beat Fortuna by unanimous decision.

This fight validated me as one of the top young fighters in Canada. The scary part was that I wasn't even close to hitting my potential yet. There was still so much room to grow and get better. I knew things were going to start getting more serious for me, and it started with getting the nod to represent Ontario at the Canada Winter Games.

CHAPTER IV

Growing Pains

Canada Winter Games, Quebec, 1983

Being chosen to represent Ontario at the Canadian Winter Games was an incredible step in the right direction. I thought I was prepared for that type of stage, but my brother wasn't as convinced. Steve knew what it took to compete at this level. He knew I barely did any road work at all and that we needed to change that. I just had no motivation to go for runs. Steve, who wasn't living at the house at the time, would run down to our parents' house and wake me up at six in the morning. I would be so pissed off, but he would eventually drag me out of bed. We would run around the neighborhood, do wind sprints at the park and sometimes we'd do some hills. I hated it at first, but after a few weeks, it became part of my routine.

The Canada Winter Games were like a miniature Olympics. They didn't just have boxing; it was all Olympic sports. I didn't really notice how big of a deal it was to be honest. I just thought it was another event, another stepping stone in my career. Every milestone was bringing me closer to the Olympic berth I so desired.

This would be my first trip out of the province and also my first-ever plane ride, so this was a completely new experience for me. When I arrived at the games, I was overwhelmed with how big it was. Everyone was right; this was a huge deal. I was happy to have my parents and Hank with me for this event because it brought me a sense of comfort I wouldn't have felt if I was alone.

Usually, I don't get too nervous before a fight, but I was feeling the butterflies before this one. Millions of people would be watching, and I didn't want to embarrass myself. When I entered the ring for my first match, the crowd was overwhelmingly supporting my opponent, Alan Brown. I looked out into the crowd and locked eyes with Hank. He nodded at me and grinned as if there was nothing to worry about. Any fear I had subsided in that moment.

Although I fought hesitantly, I was able to squeeze out a victory after the judges awarded me the unanimous decision. I carried that momentum into my second fight with Martin Cote, a native of Quebec. Again, I was able to slide past my opponent with a 3-2 split decision victory. I felt like it should have been unanimous, but at the end of the day, a win is a win. That victory punched my ticket to the finals against fellow bantamweight fighter Darren Kinequon.

After some close matches, I was done just squeaking past my opponents by way of the judge's scorecards. I wanted that gold medal, and my only remaining obstacle was standing right across from me. He had no idea what he was in for. When I got into the ring with Kinequon, I plowed right through him like a semi-truck. I used my tenacity and sheer desire to pull out a hard-fought victory. It meant everything for me to win that gold medal. Hank put me on his shoulders the moment I exited the ring and paraded me around the venue as we proudly swung the Canadian flag in victory. My parents were proud, my coach was proud and I felt pride in myself. I was the first Canadian Champion the St. Catharines Boxing Club had ever had. I could come back to the club, being the little kid among men, and show off my shiny, new gold medal. Most of the guys from the club were really happy for me, but there were some that were envious and jealous of my achievement. I began receiving even more isolated training at the gym from the trainers, which added even more jealousy. Hank threw a big BBQ at his house and invited all the fighters from the club, and some family members, to celebrate the success I had at the tournament. I felt on top of the world, and a few envious fighters weren't going to bring down my party spirit. I chugged the rest of my Pepsi and did a giant cannonball into the pool. It wasn't only a splash in their pool; I was making waves.

World Junior Championships, Dominican Republic, 1983

Since I was the Canadian Intermediate Champion, I was set to represent Canada at another big event: the World Junior Championships in Dominican Republic. Hank figured I needed to evolve my training some more, so he sent me to a club in Kitchener to train under Arnie Boehm. It was there I would meet and train with the Canadian Heavyweight Champion Lennox Lewis. Obviously, Lewis went on to be a very successful professional boxer, but this was back before all that, when he was working his way up the ranks just like everybody else.

Even though Lennox was a much larger man than me, I used him as a measuring stick. I was motivated to beat him at every turn, whether it was running the stairs, running up and down hills or just training in general. He always seemed to be a little bit ahead of me, but he continued to encourage and motivate me. I think the most frustrated I got was when we would play chess against each other. I could not beat him, not even once. He was annoyingly good at it, but it was because he was such an intelligent man. That's the thing that stood out to me the most about Lennox; he was incredibly knowledgeable and well-spoken. He was always a couple steps ahead of me, so I made it my mission to be more like Lennox when it came to mental preparation. He taught me the importance of being a few steps ahead of your opponent.

Arriving in Dominican was eye-opening for me. Never having experienced a tropical climate before, the first thing I noticed was the thick humidity. The heat was so suffocating that every activity was draining. I'm not one to enjoy sitting out in the sun, so the heat was unbearable for me. The only positive to it being so freaking hot was that it helped with cutting weight. I was fighting at 119 pounds, so I would run along the ocean with a garbage bag on to help shed some extra pounds.

Out of desperation, I was also taking water pills. At the time, water pills were legal and were used to suck the water out of your body. Running on the beach with a garbage bag and taking water pills are very dangerous ways to cut weight. But I was fighting in a weight class that I had no business being in, so the weight cut was getting more difficult.

Steve used to wear garbage bags overnight while he was sleeping to drain the water out. One time, our dad caught him doing that, ripped it off of him and told him to never do that again. Athletes have died using these types of weight-cutting methods, but it's what we did back then. Desperate times call for desperate measures.

I wasn't used to the living conditions offered to me in Dominican. The hotel rooms were very dirty and unkempt. The temperatures were so hot, and with no air conditioning, we'd have to leave the windows open all day and night. I would end up sleeping with one eye open after witnessing several giant cockroaches fly into my room earlier in the day. Needless to say, I missed Canada. I had only been there for a day, but I was ready to get on with the fights and get myself back to the comforts of home.

As I ran along the beach, I'd look out into the street corners and see the military men holding their machine guns as civilians walked around the streets. It was really humbling for me to witness that, because I wasn't very educated about different cultures. It also gave me a new perspective on many other things. I was blessed with where I was born and the opportunities that have been offered to me. As a young man, I took all that I had for granted, when in reality I am beyond blessed with the way I live in Canada.

I managed to make weight, but I knew it was going to be tough to maintain it. My stomach was rumbling continuously, but I couldn't afford to eat too much. As a teenager, that killed me. I loved to eat; I was a growing young man. The heat made my mouth so dry, and there was nothing I could do to change that. Just one drop of water would have been so satisfying.

The next day, I knocked out my first opponent in the first round. I wasn't too concerned about my first match, but I knew if I won that I would be taking on the American in my second bout. Whenever I had the chance to fight an American at this type of tournament, it was always a big deal. American fighters are the cream of the crop, the top dogs, the alphas. The amount of money Americans receive for training, traveling and other miscellaneous things is much more than any other country provides their athletes. All that funding didn't matter much in this match, because I had a height and reach advantage, and he couldn't keep up with my punches. I was on my way to the quarter-finals, and a couple matches away from becoming a world champion.

Hank was on the Dominican trip as one of the coaches. Our success in Ontario had put us both on the radar. Attending these international tournaments was beneficial to both of us. I noticed Hank was spending a lot of time working with one of Taylor Gordon's fighters. Gordon was one of the national team coaches, so he was a very influential part of boxing in Canada. It didn't occur to me right away, but thinking back on it, Hank was probably banking on this kid going back to Gordon's gym and talking about how Mr. Boone helped me with this, Mr. Boone helped me with that. That's what Hank wanted. Hank wanted to be a national coach, that was his ultimate goal on a personal level. I saw him trying to slide in there.

I planned on winning a medal. I wasn't happy just partaking in the tournament; I wanted to take the next step. In the quarterfinals I would be facing Juan Reyes, a native of the Dominican. He was a good fighter, but he was also a southpaw. I never had problems with southpaws before because I always sparred with my brother. It'd be like a right-handed fighter fighting another orthodox fighter. Whoever is smarter, stronger and quicker to the punch will be successful. It was a battle of the southpaws.

As was expected, the crowds packed the arena in anticipation of their hometown boy. There had to have been at least 20,000 people in attendance. As Reyes entered the arena, the electricity in the air was intense. The entire crowd went nuts. Even though it wasn't directed at me, it ramped me up. In sports psychology, they tell you to take the energy from the crowd and use it. Even though it was meant to be negative energy toward me, I took it and utilized it for myself.

The crowd quieted down big time after I dropped their hometown fighter twice. Both knockdowns were from quick, stiff jabs that he walked right into. He may not have been used to fighting as many southpaws as I was. He had defeated the Cuban fighter the match prior to ours, so he was no slouch. Cubans were just behind the American's when it came to boxing notoriety. I ended up defeating Reyes by a unanimous judges' decision, which guaranteed I would be taking home a medal.

After that fight, I felt like something was coming alive within me. As I kept racking up the victories against top-level fighters, I continued to get more and more confident. I was accomplishing everything I was setting out to do. My goal was to win a medal, and now I would be going home with a medal no matter the outcome of my final match. John John Molina was the only thing standing in my way from going home with the gold. That's what I thought at least. Sometimes you get in your own way though. If you want to beat a fighter of Molina's caliber, you need to be at your absolute best. There is no room for error.

I was sitting in my room sweating like a dog the night before the fight. It felt like I was trying to sleep in a sauna. My head was pounding, and I knew it was because I was dangerously dehydrated trying to maintain my weight. I had still been taking water pills every day, and my body was feeling the effects of that. It's a dangerous method, especially in that heat, and I'm lucky I didn't damage my body or, even worse, die.

Before we flew down to Dominican, they warned our entire team to not drink any of the water because it would make us sick. I was sure one drop wouldn't affect me, but I made an effort to follow the rules. I looked over at the sink, and all I wanted to do was rinse my mouth out a little bit and get some moisture on my tongue. I figured if I just swished it around for a second and spit it out, I'd be fine. Once that water hit my mouth I thought, *Well, if I just have one sip of it, I'll be okay.* So I swallowed one small gulp of tap water. I couldn't resist.

I was so dehydrated the next morning that I couldn't even pee. After the weigh-in, I just started drinking anything I could get my hands on. I grabbed some Cokes, had some orange juice, and just starting chugging them back like no tomorrow. All of a sudden, my body was like a furnace, and I became violently sick. The water from the night before gave me dysentery, and I was in rough shape. Dysentery is an illness that affects the intestines and really messes up your body.

I shouldn't have even fought, that's how sick I was. They should have just pulled me right out of the tournament. I forced myself to get in that ring, because I figured maybe I could land one and drop him. Maybe if I knew the quality of fighter I was about to face, and what he was eventually going to become, I would have bowed out, knowing I wouldn't be able to beat this guy in my condition.

I went two rounds with John John before he finished me off. It wasn't that he hit me so hard that he knocked me out, I just didn't have the energy to keep him off of me. I had zero energy to move around, my reaction time was slow and my footwork was nonexistent. My body just didn't have the strength to compete. It takes a mental toll on you when you're trying to survive an onslaught from your opponent while your body is in deep distress. At that point, you're not even focused on the match; you're more focused on the clock. I caved in. I had to resign to the fact that I couldn't beat this guy today. I took the full count, and it killed me to do that. That wasn't in my character, but that's how awful my body felt. Quitting hurts me deep down to my soul.

I was sweating so profusely during my match with Molina that Hank swore you could see the steam rising from my body. I ended up taking home the bronze medal, so I accomplished my initial goal of bringing home some accolades, but I was left wondering what could have been had I not taken a sip from the tap.

Weeks before the 1984 Provincial Championships

There wasn't much in the way of me getting to the 1984 Olympics. I was already competing against Olympic-quality talent at every tournament. The international exposure I was getting was adequate for a fighter trying to make the team, and I knew if I continued trekking down the path I was creating for myself, I would be a shoe-in.

I can recall some weeks in the summer fighting three or four times. Hank just kept scheduling me matches, loading up the car and driving me all over the place to fight. I was still quite young at this point, yet I had more experience than some Olympic hopefuls who were years older than me. Even though I had more fighting experience than most of these fighters, my life experience and maturity were constantly being questioned. My dad was always on me to be doing this or doing that. I understood he was my father, but I was getting pretty far in this boxing game without a lot of his help, so I figured I knew better.

It was about a week or two before the Ontario Championships, which is the first stage of the Olympic trials. I had a day off from training, so I thought it'd be fun to get together with my buddy Barry Stubbert and some of our other friends. We wanted to go play some ball hockey for the afternoon. I hadn't played hockey in so long, so I was kind of itching to shoot around a little bit. I dug through the garage looking for my gloves and stick, tossed some of my ice hockey equipment that I didn't need out of my bag, and off I went.

Dad asked me where I was going, because I was carrying out my sticks and hockey bag. He made a comment like,

"Shouldn't you be carrying boxing gloves and heading to the gym?"

I made a smart aleck comment back saying, "No, I'm going to go get some conditioning in and play some ball hockey." My dad suggested, "Better bring a mask with you. You don't want an errant stick catching you in the face. That'd be it; you won't be able to box." I told my dad he needed to relax. I had been playing ball hockey my entire childhood, and never once had I been cut by a stick or hit by a ball. So I didn't listen to him.

I made my way to Saints Roller Rink, which was where we always met up to play some pick-up hockey. My usual group of friends were there, but there were also a few kids that I didn't recognize. We started out playing pretty casually, but as the game went on, it started getting a little more competitive. My natural abilities were on display as I would pick up the ball and take it end to end for a beautiful goal.

It was easy to see how much better conditioned I was than these guys. I was barely breaking a sweat. To be fair, some of these guys didn't look too athletic; they were just playing for fun. This one guy, who had been playing defense for the other team, was so easy to take the ball off of. I would wait for him to gather the ball, and I would swarm him. I stole it off of him one time, and he got frustrated with me and chased me into the corner. As I was going around the net, he tried to aggressively lift up my stick to attempt a steal. I naturally moved my stick out of the way, and the guy ended up raising his stick and hitting me in the face around the eye.

I put my hand over my eye and went down on one knee. I could feel some fluid leaking through my fingers as I pressed my hand against my face. Barry ran over to check on me as everyone on the rink fell silent. "Let me see, let me see." So I moved my hand out of the way and asked, "Am I cut?"

Barry said, "Aw, Jamie, you're cut. You're cut bad." *Crap!* It was a sinking feeling. The Olympics hadn't even crossed my mind at this point. All I was thinking about was how mad my dad was going to be at me.

I had to call my father, and I was really scared to tell him what had happened. Even before I told him, I could tell in his tone that he already knew why I was calling, and he was not happy. I told him I was cut badly and needed to go get stitches at the hospital. He said, "You dummy! I told you that was going to happen. Why didn't you wear a mask? Why didn't you listen to me?" It was freak accident. I had never worn a mask before, but with so much on the line, I should have just listened and played it safe.

My dad cooled down on the phone and asked where I was so he could pick me up and take me to the hospital. I sat on the curb outside the roller rink, with a rag over my face trying to keep the blood from leaking all over me. I've never been so disappointed in myself. Boxing was so important to me, but I kept sabotaging myself. I was learning that I wasn't invincible, but I was definitely stupid.

We didn't say too many words in the car. My dad could see that I was disappointed. It felt like such a long ride to the hospital. Every stop light we went through seemed like another mile I was driving away from my dream. I stared out the window with watery eyes, praying that I could go back and revisit my choices.

My head was hanging low as I walked out of the room all stitched up. My dad was waiting outside. He put his arm around me and said, "It's okay, son. Maybe it'll heal in time." I didn't know. I couldn't spar; I couldn't train at all. I wasn't feeling very confident about my current predicament.

Hank's logic was that I was the best Canadian at that weight class, and if they wanted to have the best Olympic fighters on the team, then I should be there. He wanted the committee to make an exception for me. His reasoning was that I had won a medal at the World Championships, I won the gold at the Canada Winter Games, and I was fighting top-level fighters and beating them. Hank's pitch was that a week after the Provincial Championships, I would have a box-off with the winner, who ironically ended up being Rob Fortuna. Do they want the best for this country or not!?

The problem was that the powers that be disliked Hank. If he'd carried himself in a more politically correct manner, or just had a better reputation among his boxing colleagues, they may have heard him out. Everyone probably thought this looked great on Hank. However, it wasn't only Hank they were hurting; they were hurting me. But I recognized that this was my fault entirely.

I weighed in and everything, but they wouldn't clear me to fight with the cuts, even though they were almost healed. The opponents I would have faced were all fighters I had an unblemished record against. I would have had an amazing chance as an eighteen-year-old to make the Olympic team. One hockey stick derailed my chances.

With all the focus on the upcoming Olympics, there was nothing else really going on. I was pretty much done. I didn't know if I was going to continue boxing. I was on the fence about it for sure. I just supported my brother on his journey and cheered him on from the sidelines as he tried to make our dream come true for him.

Steve was disappointed for me. He wanted us to be the first brothers to make the same Olympic boxing team. We would have fed off each other and made Canadian history. Hank was devastated when he found out, but he was able to shift his entire focus onto Steve and try and help him qualify for the team. Although he was coach to both of us, realistically, Hank would have shown me more of the attention and affection leading up to and during the Olympics. He now had no choice but to put all his eggs in one basket, and I'm happy that was the case, because this was Steve's time. This was Steve's moment.

CHAPTER V
The Archives

Present Day

It was initially a very scary thought to even go through these boxes, but as I continue, I realize that this is my life. It was such an exciting time working my way up the ranks, winning big fights, learning from my losses and growing into a man. Obviously, I was a knucklehead at times, but I was young and naive.

My heart starts to pound heavily as I come across items dated 1988. This is why I was scared to go through this stuff. I don't know if I'm ready to reminisce on that moment of my career. I cringe anytime it's brought up to me in public. Somehow, it feels even worse facing it alone. I fear the emotions and feelings I may suffer through. Anger? Anxiety? Sadness? It's as if I'm torturing my mind. I don't have to watch the fight. I don't even need to read about the details of the actual fight. I know how I feel about the Olympics now, but it's hard for me to remember how I felt about it in the immediate aftermath. I pull out some articles with interviews I had done with several different media outlets. We even kept some footage of interviews I did with NBC and CBC. The prospect of diving into this material doesn't feed my anxiety as heavily. Maybe this will help me better understand my thought process during that time.

It was a weird couple of days. I was unsure of the proper way to handle things after the fight. A lot of the journalists asked me the same question over and over: "How would you describe your feelings after the fight?" Confused. Disappointed. Mishandled. Disgusted. There was nothing positive to take from that moment. I couldn't learn anything from it that would benefit me going forward. I learned you can't trust people. I learned how it felt to have something stolen from you. That's probably how I'd answer it today. Maybe even more aggressively depending on who I was talking to. But, during those confusing days in Seoul, I was like a deer in the headlights.

Post-fight Interviews, Seoul Olympic Games, 1988

Gerry Fogarty: Taylor, Jamie Pagendam does not want to fault the referee in any way for this loss, do you agree with that? Do you share his feelings?

Taylor Gordon: No, definitely the referee was at fault. The referee was looking around; he didn't know what was going on. The other fighter, the Mongolian, he knew what was going on. He stayed on his base and Jamie came back in from the break, lost his concentration, got hit and knocked down. It wasn't a hard knockdown, but it was a knockdown. That's what started all the problems. It's my opinion that the referee lost count of how many times the different fighters were on the floor. That can be the only explanation for what happened.

Commentator: So the Pagendam family, which failed to get a break in '84 with big brother Steve, fails to get a break again in '88 with younger brother Jamie. Here's what Jamie had to say.

Jamie: I've never been the kind of guy that ever gets the breaks, you know? I always got to do things the hard way. I just don't understand what the referee was doing in there. He sort of decided the rest of my life in a matter of seconds.

A reporter asks Jamie a question regarding his return to boxing after a small break from the sport.

Jamie: Well, the cause of my comeback, it was for a good cause and I thought I'd give it a shot to make the Olympic team, and I did. I'm happy that I'm here representing this country of Canada at the Olympics, but I'm also disappointed because I wanted to do better for the country. I just feel really bad and I apologize to everyone in Canada.

When you lose a fight while representing your country, one of the most intense emotions you feel is the fear that you let everyone down. Whether it's your family, friends or even just a fellow countryman you've never met before. When you put on your nation's colors, you're competing for everyone who's been born in that great country. It can be a lot of pressure, but it's also very humbling to have that honor.

I had to fight back tears when talking to these reporters about the bout. It was very important for me to represent myself and the country with great pride and respect. Anyone who has ever had the chance to represent their country, in any form, knows how humbling an experience it is. Even though I felt a lot of negative emotions after the fight, I made sure that I articulated myself with maturity, while still being able to show the world my frustration and passion.

Early on when I was getting interviewed, I still wasn't fully aware of what had actually transpired, so a lot of my answers may have been different had I known the whole scope of things. Right after the fight, I was thrown into the media room and was immediately under the microscope. I had no time to let anything sink in.

Interview with Wally Mathews, NBC, Seoul Olympic Games, 1988

U.S. Broadcaster: This is the scene as Pagendam headed back to the locker room, but he did make a stop to chat with our Wally Mathews.

Wally Mathews: Okay, I'm here with Jamie Pagendam; another knockout loser tonight, with another very unlikely knockout suffered by Kelcie Banks. Jamie, it was obvious you did not feel the fight should have been stopped. How badly were you hurt at the time they stopped the fight?

Jamie: I got knocked down. It was a good shot to knock me down, but I've been down many times before. Like, I'm in great shape, and I was able to get up and recuperate right away. The referee didn't even give me an eight count, he just waved the fight off and I don't understand his way of thinking.

Wally Mathews: Did he ask you if you were okay? Did he say anything to you at all?

Jamie: He didn't say nothin'. He just stopped the fight.

Wally Mathews: Is there any avenue of appeal open to you? Will your trainer try to overturn this or protest it?

Jamie: Oh, there's definitely a protest in.

Wally Mathews: Jamie Pagendam, an unhappy loser tonight. Now back to you, Marv, at ringside.

Marv Albert: That interview was conducted earlier in the day and we have been told, in fact, that Canada has filed a protest, hoping to overturn what appears to be a foul up by the referee. A decision is expected sometime on Sunday.

The interview conducted by Wally Mathews was broadcast on the American network NBC. He even made sure to highlight that Kelcie Banks was knocked out in unlikely fashion. I agree everyone expected Banks to go far in the Games, including myself. I would have really enjoyed fighting him on that stage. I can only imagine the buzz there would have been surrounding our matchup.

The interesting thing about this interview was that American broadcasting companies seldom did stories on other countries' athletes. I guess my story was too juicy to pass up. It was like the Americans took me under their wing and saw a true underdog story of how a dream was taken away from a hard-working athlete. I appreciated the love from our neighbors to the south. I could've gone without being called "an unhappy loser," though. I know I lost the fight, but I don't think any athlete likes to stand there and be called a loser in any context. Thanks, Wally.

I was trying my best to show grace during these interviews. It felt like I had to be careful with every statement I made. If this had happened to me and I was only representing myself, I know I would have handled it differently. Professional boxers are often seen speaking their minds, and it is entertaining for the fans to watch at times. Remember how well the great Muhammad Ali used to talk the talk? He trash-talked his opponents as if it were an art form. However, when you're on this type of stage, representing your flag, you're expected to show poise and respect.

Put yourself in my shoes for a second. I had just been handed one of the most controversial decisions in Olympic boxing history, then immediately had a bunch of cameras and microphones shoved in my face. It's like throwing a piece of meat to the wolves. I myself was learning new details as I went from reporter to reporter. But every reporter was asking the same question: "What happened?"

I was the biggest story early on in the Olympics. Who doesn't love a good controversy? Everyone was eating it up. In the end, I just wanted what was fair. I wanted everything to get sorted out in a just, logical way. This was a dream I'd been working toward since I was twelve years old, and I didn't want the story to end like this.

All the media attention I was getting began weighing on me. That being said, if they were interviewing me with a medal around my neck, I would be singing a completely different tune.

Unfortunately, the narrative of my story was of a fighter being victimized. I did feel good about the fact that my story was being told and not swept under the rug. I got to share my side of the story on CBC with the legendary Ron MacLean. That had to be the biggest platform I was given to tell my story.

Interview with Ron MacLean, CBC, Seoul Olympics, 1988

Ron MacLean: Joining us now, in our studio, is Jamie Pagendam. Jamie, should the fight have been stopped?

Jamie: Umm, personally, I don't think it should have been. I think the referee made a mistake ... he didn't even give me an eight count or even take a look at me.

Ron MacLean: Let's go through some of the emotions. First of all, you were extremely passionate as you spoke the night after the incident. What were your feelings going to bed that night?

Jamie: Well, I tried to go to bed, but I didn't sleep too well. Actually, I didn't sleep at all. I was kind of thinking a lot. You know, what could've happened if I would have won or what will I do now that everything's all over with? It was just a very rough night.

A very rough night was an understatement. The anxiety I felt the night before the fight didn't even come close in comparison to the butterflies eating away at my insides the night after the fight. I was just hoping to reset my mind and fall asleep, but every time I rolled over in bed, I just ended up rehashing the entire fight over again. Every time I flipped my pillow over was like rewinding the tape and watching it all over again. There was no sleep to be had as the agonizing thoughts kept my eyelids light. I would get restless lying in the same positions and, when frustration took its toll on me, I would end up sitting at the edge of my bed with my face in my palms. When you are in a dark, silent room, all you can hear is the noise you create in your own head. It was an evening of intense reflection, and it made the following day terribly exhausting.

Ron MacLean: How badly did you want this?

Jamie: I wanted it very bad. I put in a lot of time and effort into this sport and I certainly gave it my best shot. I was certainly disappointed.

Ron MacLean: It's easy to understand not really having anything to say when someone overturns the decision and you win the protest because I think that's remarkable to all of us. But, then to have it go the other way once more. Try and give me a feel for that?

Jamie: Well, at first I was very excited and ecstatic. I couldn't believe it because that's the first time it's ever happened. It's the first time I got a lucky break like that. Then all of a sudden they come back down on me again.

Ron MacLean: I know I speak on behalf of all Canadians, first in saying that you have handled this ever so well. They don't talk about humanity in terms of gold medals, they talk about it in terms of conviction. What an example you are of that. All the best.

I knew I wasn't going to stay for the entire duration of the Games. I needed to get myself home and surrounded by the people who support and care about me. None of what had transpired had really sunk in yet. There had been nothing but distraction from the time the referee made his decision to the time I got on the plane and went home.

I just wanted it to be over and done with. It was very stressful and draining, waiting for the results of the protest and, at the same time, answering the same questions over and over again with the media. For the time being, I was over it. I just wanted to get home and move past this headache. Before I went home, I did one last interview, via satellite, with Dan Matheson of Canada AM.

Interview with Dan Matheson, Canada AM, *Jamie via Satellite from Korea, 1988*

Dan Matheson: This has been a bitter, sad week for boxer Jamie Pagendam of Canada and Canadians watching at home. We have Jamie Pagendam here with us from Seoul. Kid, it looked like you got jobbed. Are you angry today?

Jamie: No, I'm learning to live with it right now. It's been a few days, so I've had a chance to really cool down about the situation.

When something newsworthy like this happens, the media likes to play the blame game. It's fair, because the only reason this situation could happen is if an individual or a group of individuals dropped the ball somewhere. The media prodded me with that question constantly. Another question I seem to get asked was how I didn't notice the fight should have been stopped earlier.

Jamie: It was a very busy round for me and it's not really my job to count the knockdowns, it's the referees' job, and the judges' job. So I was just worrying about my defense and trying to score as many points as I could.

Dan Matheson: What about the man in your corner? Shouldn't he have been keeping track too?

Jamie: Well, the referees and the judges, that's their job. It's also my corner's job too, but there wasn't a soul in the building that realized what had happened in that round until they reviewed the tape.

Dan Matheson: For the people at home who missed the fight, and what happened afterwards, the referee has been suspended for the duration of these Olympics. He will not be back in the ring. Of course, that's too late to help you. The referee blew it; we all know that. The referee blew it; the judges blew it.

I could really feel the support from Canada all the way from Seoul. Canadian broadcasters like Ron MacLean and Dan Matheson showed much more compassion while interviewing me. I appreciated the way the Canadian networks decided to tell my story and really get behind me during the days directly following my loss.

Dan Matheson: Jamie, are you going to wait around and watch the rest of the boxing?

Jamie: I haven't really decided yet. Watching the fights just makes me want to get in there myself again. What happened to me was unfortunate. People make mistakes every day in their life. The referee made his mistake, but all's I can do is forgive and forget.

After the final decision was made and sealed my fate, I was over all the media attention. Every newspaper had a take on what had happened, and every news network was showing my interviews. It was time for me to reflect on what had transpired and begin to look for some peace in the whole incident.

I enjoyed sitting at home with Fran watching some of the other Olympic events. However, even at home, I couldn't escape the noise. The phone was ringing constantly with friends and family curious about how I was doing. While I appreciated the love and support, I was still craving some silence and solitude while I dealt with processing everything. My mind needed time to find peace, but it never seemed to get any.

The Ben Johnson Scandal, Seoul Olympic Games, 1988

You could feel the excitement throughout the nation surrounding the men's 100-meter sprint. Some of the fastest sprinters the world had ever seen were competing in the finals. The most notable of the competitors were Carl Lewis of the U.S.A. and Canada's own Ben Johnson. Johnson held the title of fastest man on the planet at the time of the race. He was the biggest Olympic star in Canada, and most televisions that day would have been tuned in to see how the race was going to play out.

After all the crap that went on with me, it would have been nice for our country to get a victory in what is commonly thought to be the most prestigious event of the Games. Fran and I had it on the television live that day. I was sitting against the back wall of my rec room, praying for something positive to happen for Canada. The race was as intense as ever, but it ended with Franny and I jumping up and cheering in victory as I can only assume the rest of the nation did. Ben Johnson not only won the gold medal but he broke his own speed record, setting a new time of 9.79 seconds.

Watching Johnson's impressive showing at the Games really rejuvenated me. My spirits were immediately higher, and I felt a great deal of pride. Johnson was a national hero before he even went to the 1988 Olympics, and that race solidified his spot in Canadian hearts.

Only a few days before, everyone was talking about how this young Canadian boy got shafted at the Olympics. Now Canadians were finally able to stand up and cheer for a positive reason. The nation could focus on this triumphant victory instead of a crushing defeat. It's crazy how fast the sky can come crashing down. Two days later, the whole world stopped as it was revealed that Ben Johnson had tested positive for stanozolol, an anabolic steroid. They stripped him of his gold medal, they stripped him of his record-setting time, and they stripped Canada of a celebratory moment. Canada was left with another pit in their stomach as they once again felt cheated.

Years later, we would slowly find out that most of the sprinters in that final heat were doing some form of illegal activity leading up to the Olympics. The only one who would be penalized was Ben Johnson. This whole situation was very discouraging for me, as it was for many people.

On a personal level, it also pissed me off. I understood that it was a huge, mainstream news story involving big-name athletes. However, the reason it got under my skin was because all the Olympic media coverage transitioned to a story about an athlete cheating the Olympic system instead of my story, which was about the Olympics cheating an athlete. Of course they would take the opportunity to sweep my controversial story under the rug. My story was a black eye for the Games. The best thing that could have happened for them was for an athlete to do something such as this, to attract all the attention away.

I just thought it was unfair that I trained honestly, did all the right things, led a clean life and showed great respect to the flag, yet my story was conveniently pushed aside. I thought maybe after time had passed, my story would gain some steam again. I didn't know exactly what I wanted to come of it, but I felt like I deserved something. Unfortunately, I wasn't just pushed aside temporarily. After the dust had settled on Johnson's doping scandal, everyone had seemed to move on from my story. It was as if I had been forgotten.

All the momentum that built up around me had completely evaporated. I have no clue what would have come of it if my story did continue to build up steam. All I know is that the people who ran the Olympic Games that year never apologized or acknowledged what they did to me. I'm not surprised by that. I assume they would have had to address it eventually if the story continued to make waves in the press.

The referee never reached out to admit his mistakes and acknowledge his role in my Olympic dream being brought to an unfortunate halt. And while apologies won't change the outcome or take away my heartache, I'm just pointing out that no one cared to take responsibility. No one thought this mattered enough to make it right with me.

The only time it was ever brought up again, years later, was when one of my Olympic coaches, Ken Napper, made a joke about having to go back to school and learn how to count to three. *Hilarious*. Other than that slight acknowledgment, no one has ever been willing to admit any responsibility for taking away my opportunity. The burden lays sternly on my shoulders, as I have never felt closure.

I close the last photo album. The anxiety building up inside of me is intense. My body feels like it's vibrating from the inside out. I can't put a name to the emotion, but it's the kind that will keep me up all night. As I read the articles and watch the interviews, I can't help but put myself back in the same shoes I stood in thirty years ago. I feel like I'm heading toward another one of my classic breakdowns, but I am trying hard to resist.

I turn off the TV, which is paused on Ron MacLean's face as he signs off from our interview. I put the box aside, for now, as I try to calm down. I sit in the silence of my basement, close my eyes and sink back in my seat as I try to gather my bearings.

CHAPTER VI

Eye of the Tiger

Part One

1976

Steve Pagendam

I'm really proud of what my brother Jamie accomplished in his boxing career. It's a blessing I was able to inspire him to join this great sport, and he definitely made his mark on it. I wouldn't have thought in a million years that my eleven-year-old, sixty-five-pound brother was going to be joining me at the Port Dalhousie Boxing Club.

I guess I shouldn't have been too surprised, though; we had very similar interests. We were both athletic and had that natural desire to compete. I fell in love with boxing hard and fast. Transitioning into boxing was easy for me. I was already in really great condition from playing football and hockey, so it didn't take me long to get into the swing of things.

The reason I fell in love with the idea of boxing was because my dad had the 1976 Olympics on the television one evening. It was the first time in my life I had ever watched the Olympic Games. The way these guys moved around the ring, throwing punches at one another, was like nothing I had ever seen before.

Sugar Ray Leonard was fighting that night, and he was an impressive athlete to watch. He was so smooth on his feet and quick with his fists. My dad was lying on the couch, relaxing, when I got up and started throwing punches in the air and dancing around, imitating what I saw Sugar Ray doing against his opponent. My dad got a good kick out of that. I was even bold enough to say that one day I'd be boxing at the Olympics like Sugar. I was completely mesmerized. It was an event, a spectacle and something I wanted to try one day.

In 1977, Sylvester Stallone changed the entire course of my life when he made the film *Rocky*. I will never forget the pure adrenaline rush that hit me as I sat in the theater that evening. Everything Jamie and I accomplished in the sport of boxing would have never happened if I didn't see *Rocky* that night. Who would've thought a fictional story would have such an impact on two St. Catharines boys?

The thing that drew me so intensely to the movie was how raw and real it felt. I was impressed by the fact that this character, Rocky Balboa, had absolutely nothing when he was given this opportunity. He was just someone to fill a spot for a match that had to happen. Since his heart was so big, and the opportunity so large, he shocked the world when he rose to the occasion and gave Apollo Creed all he could handle.

A small boxing bug had already been planted in the back of my mind, so watching *Rocky* propelled me to pull the trigger. When I walked out of the theater, I knew that I was about to embark on an exciting new journey.

It wasn't long after I watched *Rocky* that I decided to join the Port Dalhousie Boxing Club as a sixteen-year-old looking for a new athletic challenge. When I walked into the gym for the first time, I was in awe. The smell of leather and sweat in the air was a scent I had never smelled before, but I immediately loved it. It looked so much like the gym Rocky trained out of. It was a small, broken-down room. They had a non-regulation sized ring, coaches doing hand pads with all the fighters and a man watching me as I walked in, my eyes beaming as I looked around the room. He introduced himself as Jimmy Neil, the gym's coach.

Jimmy asked me, "What brings you into the club, young man?" I told him I was looking to join the gym and try my hand at boxing. I had arrived just as the fighters were about to go for their warm-up run. Jimmy told me to get to work. I tied up my shoes as tight as they would go and went for a twenty-minute jog. When I came back, I couldn't find Jimmy. I thought he had left to be honest. I tapped a guy on the shoulder, and I asked him where Jimmy Neil went. The guy turned around and said, "Oh, hey Steve, welcome back." It was Jimmy, but he was now completely bald somehow. To this day I have no idea why he was training with a wig on that specific time, but it made for a memorable introduction. I never saw him wear a wig ever again.

I felt like I was making good progress in the gym. Jimmy was confident enough in my skill set to throw me in a match after only one month at the club. The fight was against a young man by the name of Shawn Ali. It's ironic because one of my favorite fighters of all time is Muhammad Ali, and, of course, my first fight was against a guy with that last name.

To be honest, it didn't feel like an official fight. For one thing, Ali weighed nearly fifteen pounds more than me. Even with many disadvantages, I was just excited to get a chance to compete. It was definitely a learning experience, that's for sure. The fight played out more like a street brawl. A lot of punches were thrown, but I don't think many onlookers would have considered what we were doing to be boxing.

In the third round, Ali landed a punch right across the bridge of my nose, and I had never seen so much blood in my life. I didn't know for sure at the time, but my nose was definitely broken. The ref stopped the fight, and Ali was declared the winner.

Jamie and my dad were both there to watch my first fight. I knew there was something wrong with my nose, but I didn't want to deal with it at the event. While I continued to sit in the crowd and watch the rest of the event, my dad came up to me and told me we had to go to the hospital to address my cracked nose.

Even though I lost the fight, this was the moment that inspired Jamie to want to box as well. What a bunch of psychos we are. Blood pouring from my nose and my face all bruised up, and that was the moment that got my eleven-year-old brother interested in the sport. Our dad agreed to letting us box, but he wasn't totally sold on the idea at first. He was even more hesitant when Jamie showed interest. You can't blame him though; Jamie was eleven years old and sixty-five pounds. Jamie joined me at the club and that set in motion our journey to becoming two of the top boxers in Canada.

A broken nose wouldn't discourage me from continuing with boxing. I was back in the club as soon as I was allowed to. This time I had Jamie following in behind me as we entered. We were the new kids on the block, and we were slowly gaining respect around the gym. It wasn't long after this that Hank Boone and his nephew Bill Hardy started coming around the club. Hank wasn't a fighter, but you could tell he loved the sport dearly. He was there most days and was acting as if he were one of the coaches.

It was nice to have someone like Hank around, especially when we were just starting out. Jimmy Neil was a good boxing mind and a solid coach, but you could see he favored one or two fighters among the rest. Jimmy focused most of his attention on Dave Morris. Jimmy believed Dave was the fighter in the club that had a chance to do something special and be somebody in this sport. When Hank saw this, he took it upon himself to motivate some of the other guys who weren't necessarily receiving the same type of attention.

Jimmy usually cornered our fights, but he couldn't make it to the Quebec/Ontario Golden Gloves tournament which took place at Toronto's King Edward Hotel in 1978. Hank and Sonny Wong worked my corner this time around. Sonny Wong would go on to become a lead boxing referee in Canada but, for now, he was just one of the guys helping out at the club like Hank.

When I competed in this tournament my record was 3-1, so I was clearly improving and getting more confident. I ended up making it to the finals in the tournament, fighting Sean O'Sullivan. In 1981, Sean O'Sullivan would go on to become the first Canadian to win a world championship when he beat three of the toughest fighting countries: Russia, U.S.A. and Cuba. He was a tough opponent, especially for my fifth-ever fight. I lost a close decision to him that night and went home with a silver medal. Hank and I became close during that tournament. He saw something extra special in Jamie and I. Hank took us under his wing and, near the end of 1978, he rallied Jamie, Billy and me to start the St. Catharines Boxing Club.

Well, life throws curve balls at you sometimes. I had just started dating a beautiful young girl named Debbie. The way I met her was pretty funny. One of my friends and I were walking down the street, a few blocks from our neighborhood, and these two girls whistled down at us from a balcony. We yelled things back and forth to each other, while my friend insisted we move along. I thought she was cute, so I convinced the girls to come down. One of those girls was Debbie. We talked a little bit, but not as much as I would have liked.

Destiny intervened a week later. I ended up seeing her again during one of my runs. Debbie was babysitting a little girl, and they were out for a stroll around the block. I took my shot and asked if she wanted to go out on a date with me. I was happy when I saw her get excited by my proposition. I told her I would pick her up at her place the next day. Immediately after I finished that sentence, I continued on with my run. After I'd been running for a bit, I realized I had no idea where she lived. So I sprinted back and, luckily, she was still walking outside. Fast forward two years later, and Debbie was having my baby. We had our first child, Aimie, in September 1979, and I married Debbie on December 1, 1979.

Everyone in my family encouraged me to stop boxing and really focus on taking care of my new family. It was a lot for an eighteen-year-old to take on, but I figured it needed to be done. We needed money for rent, food and all the other expenses that go along with taking care of a family. So ultimately I gave up training and boxing, and I began working at a factory called Moyer Depot. They manufactured vending machines, dishwashers and other appliances like that. My role there was working with sheet metal on a break machine. That was my first full-time job after graduating from high school. I saved up enough money for us to get married that December. All we had was a rented television, a hand-me-down couch from my parents and a used bed that we had to straighten out with bricks to keep level. Our rent was $280 a month and I was working for $5 an hour. We had no car to drive, so it was either public transit, bike or foot. Despite all this, we were happy because we were together.

All this was going on during a time of recession. Unfortunately, a month into our marriage, in January 1980, I got laid off permanently from Moyer Depot. I felt very down on myself. I would go as far as saying I was depressed for a few weeks. I would just mope around the house or lay on the couch feeling completely useless. It was Debbie who laid into me one day and told me to get off my lazy butt and go get a job or go back to the club. She didn't care what I did, as long as I got up and did something.

Of course, many times a week Hank would check in on me and see how I was doing. He would inquire if I was thinking about coming back around the club soon. He'd even drive up to our apartment building on his motor bike with Jamie for quick visits. He really wanted me to come back. He understood what was happening with my family, but he knew I had special talents, and he wanted to be in my corner again.

During my time away from boxing, Hank was setting up fight after fight after fight for Jamie. Hank was constantly on the phone trying to find us matches. I have never, and will never, see another man who was so good at matchmaking. He would purposely try and find fighters who were a little bit more experienced, maybe even a little more skilled than us, and it would force us to raise up our game. These matchups always challenged us to get better but left us with an opportunity to win as well. And we often would.

I had gotten a job at Gallenkamp Shoes in the Pen Centre. As much as I wanted to get back into boxing, I was having trouble comprehending how it would work. I was working a retail job, forty-four hours a week, most often working shifts that saw me closing up the store at nine o'clock at night. After taking a couple months to get used to this type of schedule, and being harassed by Hank, I eventually got back into the club and began training and fighting again. Even when I was away from boxing, the dream was always in the back of my mind that I would get back into the sport and compete at the Olympic Games. It always lingered there. I knew I had the talent needed to make it happen, but people who were looking on from the outside, like my mother and grandmother, always were skeptical about how I was going to balance time for work, family and a strenuous boxing schedule. It wasn't easy.

Between 1980 and 1982, I probably had upwards of seventy-five amateur fights. Hank was getting me fights every couple weeks, pretty much. I had to get creative with my training regimen due to time restraints with my job and family. I discussed my plan with Hank, and he gave me a key to the gym so I could train around my schedule. I'd get up at four in the morning and run three miles to the boxing club. I'd go in and hit the heavy bag, shadow box in the mirrors, skip and do tons of chin-ups and pushups. I would change out of my sweaty clothes, except my dirty underwear and socks, and then I'd take the bus back to my house around seven in the morning. I'd shower, eat some breakfast and then take the bus to work for nine. I'd work sometimes until nine at night, at which point I'd take off my tie, put it in my pocket, put on my running shoes and jog home in my dress clothes.

This busy schedule was all worth it when I could sit back and relax with Debbie for a couple hours and just chat at the end of the day. Our favorite thing to do was just sit quietly together and enjoy one another's company. I would listen to her tell me about her day, and she would do the same for me. We didn't have a whole lot, but we had love. We also had another baby on the way. In January 1982, we had our first son and named him Brad.

I felt really great about the direction my boxing career was heading. I had reason to be excited because I had won ninety-five percent of my fights, and I was getting better every time I stepped into the ring. With 1983 right around the corner, the Olympics were just over the horizon and within my sights. I knew this would be my one chance to get to the Games, so I had to capitalize on each and every moment.

In late 1982, I competed in a tournament that would open the door for me to go to the Canadian National Championships in March. This is where I would first encounter Steve Nolan. Nolan was the reigning Canadian National Champion. He was technically an Olympian as well, although he never got to compete due to the boycott of the Russian Olympics in 1980. Hank, being his usual motivating self, told me I could beat this guy:

"Steve, you're bigger than him, you're stronger than him, and you're faster than him."

The match began competitively between Nolan and I. Just in the first few exchanges, I could tell he was on another level in comparison to fighters I had seen before. During the match, I got head-butted on the nose. I don't think it was done intentionally; nonetheless, it killed and made my eyes water heavily. My vision was temporarily blurred, and Nolan was able to catch me with a shot that stunned me on the chin and knocked me down.

I didn't stay on the ground long. I was up early into the ref's counting, and I felt okay to continue. I had also gathered myself after the head-butt had shaken me up. However, the ref looked into my eyes and decided to end the fight. I was disappointed with that stoppage, but that's how the game goes sometimes. Hank told me that we'd get him next time. He knew this was going to be the guy I had to beat if I wanted to make it all the way. From that moment forward, it was engrained in my mind that Nolan was the man standing in the way of my Olympic dream.

Steve Nolan was now my measuring stick, and I couldn't wait to have another shot at him. I knew if I wanted to put on a clinic next time we met, it had to start at the gym. Hank never, ever had to call us up to get us in the gym. In fact, on one occasion, Hank was driving home from General Motors, down Queenston Street, and he drove right past me while I was doing my road work. "Atta boy, Stevie, keep it going, buddy." Hank slowed his car right down to the speed I was running and drove alongside me for a bit, motivating me while I was on my run.

I think what I liked the most about training with Hank was how much he valued sparring as a training activity. Anything that kept us actively fighting, whether it be scheduling us three fights in a week or having us constantly sparring, was what Hank found most beneficial to our progression. Our club produced a lot of tough fighters, but we earned that reputation because of the way we trained.

The club had grown substantially, adding around twenty-five more fighters to the mix. Our club was becoming more popular due in part to the fact that Jamie and I were always on the circuit. People would see us fighting at house shows, word would spread and it just kept growing from there. It also helped that this was all happening during one of boxing's most popular eras. On television, World Wide Sports would air amateur boxing on the weekends, and it was very popular in North America. Boxing was a growing sport, and we were seeing this first-hand as our gym continued to buzz.

I sparred a lot with Jamie. Hank would say that watching us spar against each other was more fun than watching our actual fights. Over time, we got so familiar with one another's style that our matches were very competitive and fluid. The fact that we were brothers and had that natural desire to one-up each other played a part in it as well. Even though we were preparing for important fights, we still ended up trying to prove to each other who had the edge. Not to mention, it's always fun watching two southpaws go at it.

Another great sparring partner I had was Rob McGregor. I'm the reason he got into boxing. When I was working a shift at the shoe store, a kid came running in and was hiding behind me. Rob came running in, looking to beat this kid up. I told Rob if he thought he was so tough, maybe he should come down to the St. Catharines Boxing Club and prove it. Lo and behold, the very next week Rob was training at the club and ended up being a very good training partner. He even went on to win the Provincial Championships a couple times before turning pro.

I also had many sparring sessions with Joe Corrigan, who is, to this day, the owner and operator of St. Catharines Boxing Club and has been for the past twenty years or so. Joe was tall and had a longer reach than anyone I sparred with, which was important for my development, as it gave me in-ring experience with taller fighters. I was going to need all the experience I could get, because my road to the Olympics was going to put me up against the top contenders in Canada.

Provincial and National Championships, March/April 1983

I made it to the finals of the 1983 Provincial Championships and defeated Johnny De Lima. Winning that fight needed to be done, because I had never experienced the National Championships before. Next year was the Olympics, so I knew I had to start getting my name into some of these more prestigious tournaments. Winning Provincials gave me the opportunity to go to Nationals in Sudbury a few weeks down the road. There, I would have the chance to potentially meet Steve Nolan again.

At the Nationals, I faced Pascal Procopio in my opening bout. Everyone told me I won the fight, except for the judges. Sometimes you just can't explain things. I can say that I hit him way more times than he hit me, but that won't change their minds after the fact. I couldn't even think back to any significant shots he landed on me. Boxing can be political at times. I took it on the chin and tried to refocus.

Jamie was in the crowd watching the fight. When they announced that I had lost, he broke down and cried out of frustration. It wasn't a close fight; I should have won. But that's what happens in sports where you are depending on a group of people to judge the outcome. I still tried to enjoy myself afterwards. I went to the back where they had a catered meal for all the fighters and officials. I rubbed shoulders with some Canadian national team members and coaches, trying to get my name out there.

One of the refs took me aside and told me how amazed he was with my ability to use my footwork to get out of situations where I was cornered against the ropes. He also told me that I won the fight, and that most people he'd spoken to shared that sentiment.

While I would get frustrated and disappointed after a loss, Hank would get fired up. Anyone who was within earshot knew how Hank felt about a controversial loss. He was always ready to go to bat for us. Even though he knew it wouldn't change the outcome of the fight, he was always digging for answers as to why a certain decision was made. He was invested in us. We were like blood to him. And in turn, we literally bled in the ring for him.

Nolan would go on to become National Champion after beating Pascal by a judges' decision. However, I still had one more chance to dethrone Nolan as National Champion at the Canadian box-offs. This event takes place in order to ensure the boxer who won the Canadian championship isn't a fluke. Only fighters who competed at the National Championships can compete at the box-offs, so I was able to try my hand. The only other fighter who put their hat in the ring was the man I just lost a controversial decision to, Pascal Procopio. The winner of our second fight would go on to challenge Nolan's standing as champion of Canada.

The fight just so happened to take place in Pascal's hometown of Sherbrooke, Quebec. I was fighting a guy who already beat me in his hometown. Call me the underdog! I dare you! If some people weren't completely confident that I should have won the first fight, I left absolutely no doubt in the second. I was accurately landing my combinations, and my movement was slick and smooth. He was getting so frustrated that he was even talking to me while we were fighting. I just kept slipping my head out of the way of punches while taking all the shots right along my collarbone and shoulder areas. He couldn't find my head, but I can assure you I found his plenty of times.

I won the fight decisively by decision. Hank was not afraid to show his passion after the fight, pounding his chest aggressively as they announced me as the winner. We both knew this was a massive win because it automatically ensured my spot on at least the Canadian national B team. The National Champion, of course, would be on the A team.

The last time I had fought Nolan was nearly two years ago. This would be a great fight to measure how much I'd improved.

Nolan was the reigning, defending National Champ, and I would have loved nothing more than to take that from him. However, this would be an uphill battle. I would fight Nolan the day after I defeated Procopio. All the punches I ended up taking on my shoulders and collarbone had tightened me right up. Hank did everything in his power to get the blood flowing and the muscles more relaxed while we were warming up. My upper body felt as stiff as a board.

I was so sore and stiff, no matter how long I warmed up for. This affected my speed, my power and my timing. Every time I threw a punch, it felt like I was throwing it with 20-ounce gloves on. I was really hoping by the time the fight actually started my adrenaline would kick in and carry me through. While I definitely felt better during the fight, it was still a tough match. Nolan was very aggressive throughout the entire bout, which changed my game plan. I decided to match his aggressiveness and meet him right in the middle and trade shots with him.

We both snapped each other's heads back multiple times. I don't like to fight this way, but, in this specific match, it felt necessary. In the end, Nolan got the better of me again and won a 4-1 judges' decision. I was disappointed but, at the same time, I also felt satisfied. This fight gave me an idea of how close I was to being up to the level I needed to be. I was now on the national B team, which meant I was going to get the much needed international fighting exposure I needed. I was hungry to keep working my way up. I had my eyes locked on those Olympic Games, only a year and a bit away now.

When I returned from Quebec, life threw many challenging decisions my way. I was informed I was being permanently laid off from my job. The gas company turned off our gas due to a major misunderstanding. When they shut off my gas, they told me it was because we hadn't made any payments on our bill in months, even though I had. They were distributing my payments incorrectly.

This pissed me off, so instead of figuring out a solution, I said, "Screw them then." We tried to survive without heat by using the stove to heat the house in the mornings, then bundling up at night. While all this was going on in my life, I was informed that the national B team would be heading to Nova Scotia for a two-week training camp, followed by a plane ride to Finland for an international tournament, also for two weeks.

This would be a whole month away from Debbie and my two very young children. My unemployment insurance hadn't kicked in yet, so we had very little money. I believe we only had $78 in the bank account. The problem was if I didn't go to Finland, I wouldn't be able to go to the Olympics because I'd have no international experience. I tried to talk myself out of it. I couldn't just leave my family to fend for themselves while I went to chase a unicorn.

I had come to grips with the fact that I had responsibilities here, and I was not going to leave. That was the mature decision I had settled on. It was Debbie who convinced me to go. She supported my dream, and she talked me back into going. Even with all her unconditional support, I felt a large amount of guilt leaving my family. I knew I had to go through these windows to open up the necessary doors that lead to the Olympics. Hank made sure to reiterate that many times as I mulled over my decision.

I felt more comfortable going knowing that my parents had offered their support, financially and emotionally, while I was gone. This relieved much of the stress I was feeling. Not all of the stress, but it gave me a sense of peace knowing Debbie and the kids had some support if they needed it. So it was settled: I was off to Nova Scotia.

International Tournament, Finland, 1983

The training camp went really well. The talent I was surrounded with was helping me develop into an even better fighter. I got the chance to spar with future professional fighters like Dale Walters and John Kelban. Our coach was Taylor Gordon, and let me tell you, he had the other coaches work us hard. This was the first time I had ever been involved with Taylor Gordon. He wasn't the coach who was going to be taking us to Finland, but he spent a lot of time working with each and every one of us.

Ironically enough, Steve Nolan's father, Frank, was one of the coaches traveling with us to Finland. Steve wasn't at this training camp, as it was just the B team participating. Coach

Gordon lived in Nova Scotia, so he hosted us at the gym he ran down there. I enjoyed the positivity he showed in his personality. I was appreciative of the technical ideas he shared with me. Although he was very nice and helpful with me, I don't think he thought much of my Olympic aspirations. knowing that I had lost to Steve Nolan.

The rules in Europe didn't make headpieces mandatory. That was different from what I was used to in Canada. This would be the first time I would compete without a headpiece but the problem was my hair was pretty long and shaggy. I had to get Debbie to wire me twenty bucks so I could get a haircut. Little did I know that it cost twenty dollars to send a wire, so this ended up being a forty-dollar haircut, and we had very little money as it was. If I had known that, I would have just shaved my head myself.

The next day we would be on a plane headed to beautiful Finland. Even though all my training was going great, I felt so lonely. I would call Debbie on the phone to make sure everything was going okay back home. It was tough to hear her voice because it made me want to drop everything and return back home to be with her.

One night, I broke down and cried just thinking about everything. It was overwhelming. The guilt I felt was intense and mentally draining. It didn't help that I had no one to talk through it with. I kept thinking about my last moments at home with my family: watching my two-year-old son playing on the swing in the backyard, Aimie sitting in the grass playing with some toys as Debbie soaked in some of the summer sun. I remember thinking to myself, *I'm going to miss them so much.*

I'd never been away from them for this length of time. I was scared to get on the plane. My life had changed so much in that last little while. While all these challenges were being thrown my way and I was chasing my dreams, I had different people telling me to get my head out of the clouds. As I sat on the plane thinking about this, 35,000 feet in the air, my head had literally never been this far up in the clouds.

I was losing faith in myself. This happens to everyone at different times. This was the first time in a while I had pulled out my Bible. For the rest of my time on the plane, and every night I laid in my room alone, I read verses and prayed. This gave me peace and restoration.

The plane landed after seven hours of straight air travel. When we got to the hotel, everyone was so exhausted and crashed immediately in their rooms. An interesting fact about Finland: In the summer months, the sun doesn't set completely; it is bright all day and all night. Midnight looks just like noon, and three in the morning is just as suitable for a beach party as any other time of the day. We all made sure to seal our blinds shut so we could avoid being kept awake by the rays of the midnight sun.

We were given time to adjust to our new surroundings and train a little bit in one of their facilities before competition began.

We were all going to get two fights here in Finland, and we wanted to be prepared properly so we could come home with meaningful experiences.

The first fight I had was with a tall fighter. I had experience fighting other tall fighters, like Jamaican Olympic team member Dewitt Frazier and American fighters Felix Vanderpool and Daryl Graham. These fighters were all six feet or taller. I had no background knowledge on the Finnish fighter I was competing against; I can't even recall his name. I knew I had enough past experience fighting tall fighters that I was going to be successful. I, being five-foot-seven, had to change my strategy around when facing fighters with this type of height and reach advantage.

For this fight, Frank Nolan was in my corner. If I'm being honest, it felt weird for me at first. However, he was very encouraging and wanted me to win my fights even though his son and I had a brewing rivalry. He gave me really great tips in the corner and was very insightful.

When the match started, I moved around, trying to find my angles. Thirty seconds into the first round, I hit him with a shot that dropped him to one knee. The ref took a look at him and stopped the fight right then and there. We were both shocked. I was shocked with how quickly the fight was over; he was shocked with what I just hit him with. The Finnish boxing contingent was very upset with the ref's decision to stop the fight so quickly because this guy was their champion in Finland.

I was supposed to fight a different fighter for my second fight, but the Finnish officials called my win a fluke and wanted there to be a rematch instead. Every other Canadian there faced a new challenger, while I fought the same guy again in an effort to prove that my win was legit.

So we met in the ring again, and we had a more competitive first round. We were both landing some punches, but there wasn't a whole lot of action for the most part. The second round ended any talk of a fluke. I landed a jarring body shot and followed that up with a hard hook that dropped him. For the rest of the second round, I chased him around the ring as he wobbled in retreat. I snapped my jab from all angles. Once I was able to corner him against the ropes and hit him with a flurry of combinations, the ref was forced to step in and take him out of his misery.

Man, I was so excited. Word got back home that I had won both my fights through a wired message. Hank would receive the messages and relay the information to the family. I felt as though the training I did with the B team was very beneficial to my progression. The way they trained was more intense, so I planned on upping my daily training regimen to include running up hills and, overall, more endurance training.

This trip to Finland gave me the confidence I needed to believe in myself and in my ability to reach the Olympics. The Games were in just over a year, so I didn't have much time to prove myself. It was do or die. Every moment, every fight and every training session was critical.

As the plane finally landed back on home soil, my excitement rose through the roof. Finally seeing Debbie and the kids after a long month away was going to give me so much joy. I couldn't have walked off that plane and through the tunnel any faster than I did.

The second I walked through the gate, I saw Debbie standing there with my parents. Her skin was tanned from the summer sun, and she had a brand-new, blue sundress on. I ran up to her and hugged her right off of her feet. This reunion made the whole trip seem worth it, but I definitely wasn't keen on doing it again.

I was surprised to see her wearing a new dress, knowing our financial situation was not great. I asked her about it. Since I had made the Canadian national team, they gave me carded status. That meant that all my training expenses were covered by the government. It was a blessing from God. They were going to send us $450 every month. While I was away, they sent Debbie a check for $900. I was able to pay the gas company and some of our other outstanding payments.

Training with a highly skilled group of fighters taught me some valuable things in terms of how I should be training if I wanted to make the Olympic team. At the age I was at, and with other responsibilities in my life, the 1984 Olympics were my only shot at living out my dreams. I got Hank to push me every time we trained, and I made sure to get lots of road work in, including many large hills. I knew I had the heart and desire to get to the Games, and I knew exactly who I had to beat in order to get there. The chapter between Steve Nolan and me had only just begun.

CHAPTER VII

Eye of the Tiger

Part Two

Steve Pagendam

I went into every fight telling myself I was the underdog. It didn't matter who I was fighting or where I was fighting; I went into each fight with that mentality. It was me against the world, and I was motivated to prove all my doubters wrong. This mindset kept my hungry. I was starving for my fights.

   I spent most of the next six months fighting as much as I could. This included some international fights in Ireland and the United States. I was in the absolute peak shape of my boxing career, and I was getting stronger every day. This, in turn, increased my confidence with each training session and each fight that went by. There were only six weeks until the National Championship Olympic trials, so I was hitting my stride at the perfect time.

It was also around this time, in January, that I got hired at General Motors. Working a full-time job, which included a lot of shift work, created new challenges to overcome. These next six months were going to prove if I really wanted this or not. I wouldn't let it get in my way though. There was no time for anything other than work, dedicated training and, of course, family time mixed in whenever I could.

I was running to and from work every day, no matter if it was a morning shift or a midnight shift. I knew the best places for hill training, and I would choose a route to work where I could stop for ten minutes to run up and down a challenging incline. We didn't have a car, so if I ever needed to pay a hydro bill or a gas bill, I'd throw on my track suit and I'd run there. It sounds ridiculous, but it was what I had to do. Rocky used to gulp back raw eggs in the morning before his workouts, so I began this morning tradition as well. This was the most serious I had ever been about boxing and the most focused too.

Just prior to February, Canada was slotted to face the U.S. Olympic team as a pre-Olympic tune up. It was meant to be the Canadian national A team facing the U.S. national A team. There was a lot of excitement around these fights, and they were set to be televised.

Steve Nolan, who was on the A team, for some reason or another couldn't make the fight that night, so I was asked to take his spot on the card. Willie Dewitt and Sean O'Sullivan were the marquee fighters on Canada's team, and it just so happened to be in Dewitt's home province of Alberta. The venue was jam-packed with fight fans. Hank was excited to be working my corner, because it was going to give good exposure to the St. Catharines Boxing Club and both of us individually.

We had a lot of people excited to watch the fight back in the Niagara Region, including many of the General Motors employees who knew I worked at the plant. I was ready to show off my boxing skills on national television.

The beginning of my fight was fairly close until the end of the first round when I got cut over my eye. During the round's break, Hank was trying everything possible to get the bleeding to stop, but it just kept pouring out like a burst pipe. I could hardly see and was taking shots I normally would avoid. The ref kept stopping the action to check on my cut while blood was literally covering my entire face. The ref eventually called the fight in the second round because there was just way too much blood.

I was so embarrassed to have my first nationally televised fight be stopped when it was supposed to be my chance to shine. After the outcome of that fight, I swore to myself to never be embarrassed like that again. I put a whole new attitude toward my boxing, and it was ultimately the final piece of my puzzle. I had created the perfect storm, and I was ready to strike. I was pissed off, and I never wanted my heart to feel like this again.

I had six weeks to heal up before the biggest weekend of my career. If I wanted to make the Olympics, I needed to win the National Championship. I knew who this road went through. Every time I woke up at five in the morning to run, I thought about him. Every time I wanted to quit, I thought about him. Every single time I sank my fists into the heavy bag, I was thinking about him.

The month leading up to the fight, Hank drilled the same sentences into the fibers of my brain over and over again. You're bigger, you're faster and you're stronger. The more you tell yourself something, or in this case have someone tell you, the more you start to actually believe it. It got to the point where I wholeheartedly believed without a doubt that I was faster and I was stronger than Nolan. I'd already lost to him twice, but he'd never fought this version of me before. I had the experience behind me now, and my training had never been so focused.

The Steve Pagendam that had those two loses on his record no longer existed. He existed if only to be a reminder of what I had been working toward for that past year. I wanted it so badly that it made me want to cry just thinking about it. This fight wasn't just for me; it was for my family who had sacrificed so much just so I could chase my dream. Without Debbie's unwavering support, I wouldn't have been able to pursue this.

Canadian National Boxing Championships, Trois-Rivieres,

Quebec, March 1984

For the most important fights of my career, I brought my father and Jamie. It was important for me to have them there for support. My dad has always been there for his boys, every step of the way. His love and passion for what we did, no matter what it was we were doing, was the best example of what a father's love for his children should look like. Like every other time I've needed him, he was there for me that weekend.

Jamie, who should've been competing this weekend too, wasn't medically cleared to fight. He got a gash on his head from playing a pick-up hockey game a couple weeks before. I was happy he still wanted to come support me. Hank allowed him to stand in my corner during the fights.

My first fight was against a fighter from Toronto. I picked him apart for an easy 5–0 judges' decision. That victory stamped my ticket into the finals against the man I'd been waiting to sink my teeth into for almost a year. I would be fighting Steve Nolan the next day. I had to control myself. Just thinking about the opportunity had my adrenaline rising so fast that it felt like I was going to implode. I was scared this would drain my energy, so I forced myself to relax. I sat in my room, listening to my dad speak to me. Even he couldn't resist hyping up the fight, though.

When I found a peaceful moment in the evening, I closed my eyes and visualized how I wanted the fight to go. I could see his face so clearly in my mind. It's the only face I wanted to see across the ring from me. I wonder if he thought about me sometimes. He knew we were fighting that next day, but he had no reason to think about me the way I thought about him. I made it my mission to change that. I wanted to make sure that after this fight, I was burned into his brain.

I'm not going to be embarrassed again. I'm bigger, I'm faster and I'm stronger.

I woke up with a purpose that next morning. My body felt loose, my mind felt free, and I was well rested. It was these small details that gave me that extra confidence boost. I had no excuses this time around. I knew I was just going to let it all hang loose. The fight was to take place at two in the afternoon, which was earlier than I was used to. I got to the facility sooner rather than later because I was itching to get my warm-up in and get into fight mode.

This was the most fun locker room environment I had ever created. I was changing it up, and I didn't give a care in the world. Today wasn't about traditions or superstitions; today was about breaking all of that and creating a new outcome. I pressed play on the boom-box and began dancing like I was a kid again. Michael Jackson's *Thriller* album echoed through the room as I floated around, sweating like crazy. I moonwalked across the floor as I

112

held my hands up in my fighting stance. Jamie turned up the speakers when "Beat It" came on, and it only made me dance harder. I felt like this was my day.

Everything looked exactly how I had pictured it in my mind. The ropes, the mat, the faces in the crowd all felt extremely familiar. It was like I had been here before. Then out came the defending National Champion, Steve Nolan. The clear favorite in this match was Nolan, just based on the fact that he had years and years of international fights under his belt—not to mention he'd beaten me twice already. Enough talk already. Fighting is done in the ring, not by the analysts. I looked across the ring and finally saw the face I'd been dying to see. A face I was determined to rearrange. Jamie put my mouth piece in for me, Hank gave me slap on the back and the bell sounded.

Just like in the locker room, I was dancing around the ring as if the music was flowing through my veins. I was snapping my jabs between his guards continuously as I picked him apart. It felt like I was able to land my punches whenever I wanted and, at the same time, avoid most of his attacks. Hands down, I won the first round. Hank couldn't believe what he was seeing in there. Hank was always confident in us, but this time around he was in shock. He wasn't shocked so much that I was winning, but how I was winning. "You're out boxing him Steve. You're just beating him up in there. Keep it up."

The second round was more of the same. I just kept pounding him with my cleanest and most accurate strikes. I was drilling him with powerful body shots, followed up with sharp shots to the head. To be completely candid, it felt like I was in there with a kid. I was dismantling the National Champion, and I didn't plan on letting up one bit. If Nolan underestimated me at all before this fight, he was definitely changing his tune after this performance. The measuring stick I had set for myself was right in front of me, and I was pounding it deeper and deeper into the ground. When I made my way back to the corner, Jamie was fired up. Hank was rubbing my shoulders and feeding me more motivating words. I knew what I had to do, though.

If you could measure confidence, mine would have broken the scale. I would have loved to be a fly on the wall in Nolan's corner. What could they possibly be talking about over there? The third round started, and I continued my dominance. I willed myself to this performance. I just had to win this match. Part way through the round, I caught Nolan with a punch that staggered him enough for the ref to step in for the eight count. My brother was yelling and screaming in the corner with excitement. Unfortunately, during this tournament, there is no coaching or any kind of communication allowed from the corner. Before the ref began the count on Nolan, he turned to Jamie and issued my corner a warning. This gave Nolan time to recover, but not enough time.

I went back in and started landing, and eventually I hurt him badly with another right to the chin. I was going in for the kill. I could feel the ref getting ready to show Nolan mercy by ending the fight. The ref did in fact stop the action, but it was again because Jamie was freaking out in the corner during my onslaught. I was literally seconds away from finishing him, and Jamie got warned again. The funny thing was, right as the ref turned to give another warning, Jamie realized that what he was doing was hurting me, and he ran out of the corner toward the back of the room like a dart.

Again, Nolan had time to recover and the match ended without a finish. The judges gave me a 5-0 decision in what was the most satisfying victory of my career. I would go on to win my next fight, the gold medal, and the title of National Champion in my weight class. This was the best weekend I ever had in boxing. Nolan and I ended up winning fight of the tournament, and I went home with the huge honor of winning fighter of the entire tournament.

Next on the road to the Olympics were the box-offs. It was the same scenario as the previous year, except this time I was the National Champion, and someone would be trying to dethrone me. If someone did end up beating me, though, I would still remain the National Champion until we had a final match to determine the true champion. I didn't plan on letting it get that far. If I could win this next fight, I'd be all but guaranteed a spot on the 1984 Canadian Olympic Team.

The box-offs were to take place in Nova Scotia, so I thought it'd be nice to bring Debbie with me so she could visit her brother, Jim. Jim had moved down east when he joined the Navy. It was exciting for me to have her there for a very important fight. Jim was a very good host, showing us all the cool areas of Nova Scotia. Exploring the beautiful city together with my wife and brother-in-law kept me relaxed and loose leading up to the day I would fight.

The night before my fight, the three of us went to the first round of the box-offs, which saw Nolan take on the Toronto-based fighter I beat in the first fight at Nationals. The winner would face me the next night. Nolan dominated him and eventually knocked him out in the first round in devastating fashion. Immediately after his dominating victory, he found me in the stands and glared at me from the ring. He stared me down, almost as if to say "you're next." It was at that point the rivalry seemed to officially become just that, a rivalry. It was no longer one I was creating in my head, but a true rivalry. I had defeated him, and he now saw me as a real threat to his Olympic dream. I was trying to take away something that he had been groomed for since 1979.

I felt confident that I was going to be able to build off my last performance against Nolan. Although there was no Michael Jackson music playing this time, I still felt the swagger in the locker room. I had the best kind of butterflies that day, and they followed me as I confidently strutted toward the ring with my coach. It was time.

This was going to be a much different battle from our first tilt, but I was prepared for anything at this point. Debbie gave me a nervous smile as I looked across the crowd one last time before I focused all my energy on retaining my title as National Champion. Nolan had a different look in his eyes than the last time. He resembled a bull being cooped up in his cage right before his release onto the matador. Nolan put his hands up high and just charged at me as if I were wearing red.

While I like to dance around and use my footwork and speed to pick apart an opponent, I found myself backing up. I did not feel like running around the whole match, looking like I was constantly on the defense. My tactics needed to change, so I also put my hands up high, and we began just taking it to each other in the center of the ring. With both of our feet planted, we dug in and boxed like warriors. I didn't give him any room to breathe. Literally, we could feel each other's breath on our bodies as we stood close in our stances. Being in a tight space like this during a fight limits your arsenal to short hooks and what people like to call dirty boxing. Not dirty in the sense that it's illegal, but dirty in the sense that it doesn't look nice.

Midway through the fight, you could tell Nolan was getting frustrated with the gritty style we were fighting. This is the style he was trying to fight; I was just combating it by matching his style. I was crowding him, and he was getting pissed that he wasn't able to get any clean shots off. Every punch was thrown from the inside. Nolan pushed me away from him with a violent shove.

The next thing that happened was the only time I've had this happen to me, and I thought about this for a long time. I've had fighters talk to me in the ring before, but that wasn't the reason it was unusual. What Nolan said was, "Come on, Steve, box." I can still hear it clear as day when I play it back in my mind. I've never had another fighter tell me how to conduct the way I was fighting. I found it very strange and kind of desperate. Not that he needed to be; it was a very close fight that could've gone either way at that point. I'm guessing he didn't expect me to be able to adjust so quickly to what he was trying to do; he wasn't prepared for that. It didn't change the way I was going to finish the match though. If it ain't broke, don't fix it.

This was a much closer fight than our previous bout. I felt like I was doing enough to win, but they were probably saying the same thing in his corner. Hank was telling me I was winning the fight. He never told us that so we would relax. It wasn't about giving us a sense of peace or an excuse to coast. The man always wanted us to keep our hands up and continue to press. Hank knew this third round was going to be active and fast-paced. This round could decide the fight.

Every punch in the third round was thrown with meaning and purpose. There was no fluff being tossed around. While most amateur fights are more about scoring points, we were two men standing toe-to-toe trying to knock each other out. This felt very much like a professional fight. The stakes were high, the emotions were high, and the fans were split.

Near the end of the very busy third round, Nolan clipped me cleanly on the chin, and everything went black. Hank and I talked about it after the match privately. He said he saw how hurt I was after that shot. I don't remember this, but apparently, out of instinct, I ducked my head down and Nolan just missed a huge follow up shot that would have most certainly put me on dream street. It had to have been instinct because I couldn't see or hear anything in those moments. I regained my vision and continued on. No one knew that punch dazed me: not Nolan, not the ref. I didn't put on that the shot had hurt me at all, even though I was in big trouble. We finished the fight with another close round. They were all close rounds but I felt like I was the busier fighter in all three rounds.

Hank was certain I had won this fight. Dennis McNeil, Sr., who was also working my corner that night, said the same thing as Hank. I was disappointed when the judges awarded Nolan with a 4-1 decision. Hank shook his head, calling B.S. Nolan was pumped because his Olympic dream was still alive. This ultimately became a best two-out-of-three series now, with the rubber match deciding the true National Champion.

There's a lot of politics in boxing, and I'm not saying that he didn't deserve to win that fight, but Hank and I could see something unraveling. They didn't want me to be National Champion. They had spent years pumping money and resources into Steve Nolan with the hopes of him representing Canada. Nolan had built relationships with everyone involved with the national A team. He was their guy. "They are going to take this away from you, Steve." Hank was pissed. I tried not to let it bother me. It kind of made me feel like Rocky a little bit. With an underdog mentality, I was going to find a way to beat the odds and make it my moment.

After the fight, I met Debbie back at the hotel, and we got ready to go meet Jim for a nice dinner. There were many people I recognized from the boxing event at the restaurant. The technical director of Boxing Canada, Matt Mizerski, called me over. He had a European accent, and he always seemed to like me whenever we would cross paths. He said something that rubbed me the wrong way that night, though. "Steve, what are you doing? This is the Olympic year. You bring your wife on a big tournament like this? You can't be having distractions." I defended myself, though. I believe I won that fight, and I told him that. If anything, having her there helped me. What he said really upset me mostly because I knew Debbie was close enough to hear, and I didn't want her to feel a certain way about it. On the plane ride home, she asked me if she was a distraction. Not in the slightest; you will always be my strength.

Fight clubs were gearing up for the Olympics, so there wasn't much sparring going on in the summer months. Hank knew of some clubs over the border in Buffalo that we could go to get some sparring in. It was about a 45-minute drive, but it was worth the trip in order to stay in fight shape. There was one scary time at the border when we were coming back from Buffalo. They made us pull the car over for an inspection. They brought the dogs out, and they ripped apart the entire car, front and back. They went through that vehicle with a fine-toothed comb. Meanwhile, I was just sitting there, drenched in sweat from my workout, looking at Hank, wondering what the heck was going on. They kept us there for a long time before finally letting us leave. I was confused, but Hank assured me it must've just been a misunderstanding. We only went over the border a couple more times after that for sparring.

Everyone I talked to was excited for me to win this next fight against Nolan and ensure my spot in the Olympics. But my dad and I had a serious chat, and he knew how this was really going to go. Nolan had been National Champion since 1979. He was on the Olympic team in 1980 that boycotted the Olympics. They'd invested too much into Nolan not to take him to the Olympics. My dad said, "They're not going to let you go to the Olympics, son. Even if you beat him, they'll give him the decision.

Even if you beat him by decision, they'll still take him to the Games." It wasn't fair, but it made sense.

It was unlikely they would take me over him because of his international experience and his world ranking. It's not fair, but it's the politics of this sport. Obviously, I wanted to go to the Olympics, but there was another thing that was bothering me in the back of my mind. I didn't want anybody to be able to say that my one victory over Nolan was a fluke. The one where I dismantled him for three straight rounds was the most satisfying win of my career. I did not want anybody to be able to take that away from me. I don't want Nolan to ever be able to justify it by saying he just had a bad day. My dad finished our conversation by saying, "Son, you know you have to knock him out if you want to go to the Olympics." Nolan had never been knocked out before.

The final fight of our rivalry would take place in the beautiful city of Vancouver, British Columbia. A rivalry that almost seemed too perfect the way it lined up. We're both named Steve and have the same birthday of February 10th. Whichever one of us went to the Olympics would be the only member of the team to be married with children at home. We both had full-time jobs while pursuing this dream. Two men, with the same dream, in the same sport, at the same weight, find themselves in a match that will determine their future. Both our lives would take different courses after this match. Hank knew from the beginning it was always going to come down to this. Steve vs Steve.

The hotel room in Vancouver was pretty much a glorified closet. The room consisted of a bed, a sink and a mirror. I spent almost all my time by myself in this room, shadow boxing in the mirror while I tried to swallow my stress and anxiety. This time I wasn't dancing around to "Beat It." I wanted this so bad, and it was putting me under an immense amount of pressure. This was the culmination of six years of hard grinding and intense dedication.

Hank knocked on my door, as it was time to go weigh in. Steve Nolan was down there, and every national team member was hanging around him like groupies to a rock star. He had everyone in his corner giving him back rubs and making sure he had everything he needed. Dale Walters, who made the 1984 Olympics, was from B.C. and was housing Nolan during his stay. He even set it up so Nolan could train at his facility during the week. Dale Walters went on to win the bronze medal at the '84 Olympics in the bantamweight division. Hank and I walked up to the scale, and I was right at the weight I needed to be.

Seeing that whole group down there reiterated to me that it was me against the world. It almost felt like I wasn't supposed to be there, like I was intruding. The only person I had backing me in the whole place was Hank Boone. After the weigh-in, it was back to my room to meditate on my match the next day.

I admired Hank's ability to exude confidence. He wanted to swim with the big fish, and he played that part beautifully. He didn't know what the outcome was going to be, but he was always willing to put it all on the line to get his fighter's name out there. The night before my fight with Nolan, Hank was down in a private lounge area with many of Canada's boxing officials, the judges, the refs and some of the other fighters' training staff.

Hank told them how he felt, and he didn't leave anything he said up for interpretation. "We know how it's going to be. Nolan is the guy; they will make sure Nolan gets his spot on the Olympic team." Everyone brushed Hank off. But everyone's ears pricked up when Hank made a bold claim. "My boy is gonna beat Nolan tomorrow. Steve will not only win, he will knock Nolan out." He was the only one in that room that even believed a shred of that. Hank wholeheartedly believed in me as a fighter, and he stood up for me all night in that room. He made his claims and his guarantees until the sun rose. Meanwhile, I was in bed trying to sleep, but the echoing in my head kept me up. *You can't lose this fight. You can't lose this fight. You can't lose.*

I got myself situated in my locker room a few hours before I was to face off with Nolan. I sat there for a bit trying to visualize the fight, but I was sick of dwelling on it. I decided to leave the facility and go for a walk to clear my head. I had been cooped up in my room the last few days, doing nothing but thinking about the fight. I needed some fresh air. I came across a park midway through my walk. As I turned the corner, I was met with the majestic scene of mountains in the distance. The sky was blue, and the sun was shining through the openings between the mountains. In this very moment, I felt still and calm. I couldn't get over how wonderfully powerful these mountains were.

As I continued walking, I came across a track where I saw a group of children running around. I leaned up against the fence and watched them run around for a bit. As I watched closely, I realized that these kids were part of a special needs program. They were enjoying life with big smiles on their faces, making each other laugh with joy. Even though they may have been going through challenges, they were embracing the day. For the first time in a while I felt like all the pent up tension, emotion and anxiety, that at times had me on the verge of crying, left my body. I thought, *Look at the opportunity I have. It's like God brought me here for a reason.* I thought about all my blessings and how much I had been given. This moment I was about to have with Nolan should be embraced; it shouldn't be feared.

The locker room was silent. It was just Hank and I as he secured my fists in the hand wraps. I looked down at his shaking hands and remembered how important this was to him too. He had invested many years into my boxing, and he had always believed and stood by me no matter the circumstances. He built an entire club around us with the belief that we would one day be champions. Who knows where I would be right now if this man didn't put his money where his mouth was.

We didn't exchange any words for what seemed like an hour. It was just pure, uninterrupted silence. He held up the hand pads for a warm-up, but with every combination it seemed like either I was off or Hank was off. I put my hands down and said, "Hank, forget it. I'm ready. We don't need to warm up." It wasn't flowing. We looked like two people who had just met and tried to do hand pads for the first time. I think it was nerves and butterflies. For the duration of the time, I just sat down, closed my eyes and soaked in the silence.

Even though the ring was surrounded by many fans, it felt as silent as the locker room, as silent as the tiny closet they had me sleeping in, and it felt as calm and as still as the backdrop of mountains in the park. I was done with all the outside noise; this was now solely between Nolan and I. It didn't matter what the so-called experts had to say, it didn't matter what the other fighters had to say, it didn't even matter what our coaches had to say; the fight was between us, and there was a lot on the line.

Right before the match was about to start, I felt this aggressiveness come over me. It was like a switch turned on in my head. I looked up at Hank and he said, "Let's give it to this guy one last time." I looked across the ring at him, and thought, *I'm bigger, I'm faster and I'm stronger*. I knew I just had to let it all hang loose in there. This was the last time I would ever get a shot at going to the Olympics and the last time I would ever get a shot at beating Nolan. But I knew I couldn't just beat Nolan if I wanted to go to Los Angeles in July; I had to leave no doubt.

Every punch I threw in the first round was thrown with ill intent. I was rocking this guy backward and using my footwork to stay out of his range. Even the jabs I was throwing were meant to hurt this guy. I was throwing my uppercuts from the outside, as opposed to the inside where you normally see them. They kind of looked like upward jabs. I had no idea how he was feeling during the match, but after looking back on the fight and watching the tapes, it appeared as though I was rocking him with every punch I landed. All I knew was that I was hitting him with some of the hardest punches I had ever thrown.

In the second round, it was more of the same. I felt like I barely got hit in the first two rounds of action. I had hit this guy with some of my best combinations, but he still just wouldn't drop. Nolan was fighting very defensively and protecting his chin the best he could. I knew if I could land a clean shot right on his chin, the match would be over. I was looking for the opportunity to throw a knockout punch but, like I said, they are hard to come by.

As I went to my corner between rounds, I knew I was dominating the fight, but it wasn't enough. I felt some of the pressure come back to me. Knowing that I had to knock him out within the next three minutes was creeping into my mind and creating stress. Adrian Teodorescu, who was helping Hank in my corner, leaned under the ropes and got really close to me. "Stevie, don't be stressed. You're doing everything perfectly. Just keep doing what you're doing, enjoy the moment and it will come together for you." Although Adrian was not someone I was around very often, that simple speech brought my mind back to a state of peace and reminded me to embrace the moment ahead. Hank slapped my mouth guard back in and, as I confidently stood up from my stool, he told me to not leave anything to chance.

I noticed in our previous fights how intelligent a fighter Steve Nolan was. He came up with game plans and adjustments during the match after analyzing his opponents and implemented them when the opportunity arose. I thought I could potentially goad him into a certain punch so I could open him up and land my thunderous hook. Twenty seconds into the third round, I threw a telegraphed slow right hook. Before I threw it, I stepped back out of range. It was a half-assed punch, meant to give him a look. I knew Nolan would see the huge opening I was giving him. The punch he should throw in this situation would leave me the opening I needed to land my perfect shot.

It was risky, but I needed to make something happen. If I was to time this correctly, and he played into it, this could be a huge moment. Soon after I threw the original, telegraphed hook, I moved in closer and did it again. This time I followed it up by throwing a straight left punch right down the middle. I didn't plan on taking a shot during this exchange, but Nolan hit me with one of the hardest shots I've ever felt, and it stunned me really bad. The punch landed so hard that it spun my head right around as if I were an owl. I had instant ringing in my ears as time seemed to slow right down, and I knew I was in deep trouble. When my head snapped back I was expecting to be rocked with a follow-up shot, but there was nothing. Instead, I was looking at my rival, my biggest obstacle, and the best fighter that I ever had the chance to share the ring with, lying on the ground.

The ref was counting, but he shouldn't have been. Nolan was literally grasping at the clothing of the referee, desperately trying to regain his footing. The ref gave Nolan every opportunity to get up by giving him a full ten count. But it was official: I had knocked out Steve Nolan.

CHAPTER VIII

Eye of the Tiger

Part Three

Steve Pagendam

Everything was moving in slow motion. I don't remember hearing the crowd; I don't remember hearing the ref counting. All I remember is feeling my heart pounding in my chest as I watched Nolan desperately try to regain his footing. It was to no avail. The ref waved his hands to signify the end of the match and all the surrounding sounds rushed back to me like a giant wave crashing against a pier.

Excitement was written all over my face as Nolan and I stood at the center of the ring waiting for the referee to make it official. After the match, Hank was waiting for me outside the ring. He was jumping up and down, and I ran to him. I jumped up so high into his arms that he caught me by my shins, and I almost flew right over his shoulder. I'm lucky I didn't injure myself during that celebration, but I was just too pumped up.

Dale Walters had everyone over for a post-fight dinner, including Nolan. Nolan was a good friend of Dale's, so you can imagine how uncomfortable I felt sitting at a table two seats away from Nolan. During the dinner, Nolan piped up and said, "Hey Steve, you're a dirty fighter, eh." I just looked at him for a second and said, "How am I a dirty fighter?" Nolan quickly replied, "You were twisting my arms, trying to break them. You're dirty, man." He wasn't completely wrong about that; I did crank down on his elbows whenever he'd hold onto my body, but then don't hold onto my body. I just said, "You kept holding on to me, I was just trying to get out of the clinch." We didn't say much more to each other that night.

A month after the Nolan fight, I still wasn't named to the Olympic team. Hank was constantly in communication with the officials in charge of naming Olympic team athletes. He was putting pressure on them to make a decision, while constantly working whatever angles he could to try and swing them in the right direction. Nolan couldn't go to the Olympics because I knocked him out, which meant he was issued a 90-day suspension from competition.

At the end of May, I finally got notified of their decision. The reason it took so long was because in order to qualify for the Olympics, you must rank within the top sixteen in the world for your weight class. Since I had a lack of international experience, I did not rank. However, they decided, since I knocked out Nolan, I would take over his ranking, along with his entire international record. With that being said, I was officially Olympic bound.

While everyone was incredibly inviting, I could tell there was some awkwardness toward me. These guys had been training and competing internationally with Nolan for the better part of two years. Now all of a sudden, I was there instead. At the end of the day, boxing is an individual sport so, whether they liked it or not, it didn't really affect me.

I enjoyed training in Vancouver; it was such a beautiful environment. We did a lot of training outside, and the backdrop was breathtaking. It lost its magical appeal after a few days, and I was ready to go to Los Angeles and just get this thing going. I had been training for this for eight years, and I was ready to unleash everything I had pent up inside of me.

A couple days before we were to leave for L.A., the entire team, including coaches and all other additional personnel, were ushered into an auditorium. I wasn't too sure what to expect, but apparently they were going to show us some videos to hype us up.

The video they showed made me want to curl up into a ball and disappear. It was a segment that was going to air on CBC, profiling a few of Canada's boxers who were hopefuls to bring home medals. The interviews were filmed a few weeks before I fought Nolan for the third time. But lo and behold, there was Steve Nolan on the big auditorium screen talking about his chances at the Olympics.

The kid was so cocky during the interview. "Look at my face, not a scratch on me. I've been all over the world, been in hundreds of fights and look at my face; no scratches." They filmed him at his workplace, hanging out with his wife and kids and training at his gym. Everybody knew how awkward this was, but no one said a word. After his portion of the video played, there was a little message blurb that popped up on the screen that said something along the lines of "Due to unknown personal reasons, Steve Nolan will not be competing at the 1984 games." It didn't say anything about me taking his spot from him by knocking him out. In fact, it didn't mention me at all. I sank deeper into my chair and just prayed for this to end soon so I could go back to my room.

Although I was beyond ecstatic to have earned my spot on the Olympic team, I always felt bad about taking that away from Nolan. I know how hard you have to scratch and claw to get into that position. I especially know how hard it is to accomplish this feat with a wife and kids at home and a full-time job. Steve Nolan has my utmost respect. I felt like I was fighting for both of us at the Olympics. I took his opportunity, so I didn't want to squander mine.

Summer Olympic Games, Los Angeles, August 1984

Prior to the Olympics, a few fighters took a stand and demanded they get to bring their own coach to work their corner for the Games. Since they were important fighters to the team, Canada's boxing officials gave in and allowed it. This set a precedent, which opened the door for Hank to work my corner at the Games. He wasn't able to stay in the Olympic Village with me, but he got a room close by. Not only was I living out my dreams, but now so was Hank.

Once we landed in L.A., I was hit with a rush of adrenaline. The thought of competing on this large stage, and thinking about what I had to accomplish to make it here, fired me up. I wanted to make the most of this opportunity. The thoughts began running through my mind. *What kind of draw am I going to get? What are my chances of winning a medal? Who will I fight first?* Even as I think back on it now, it feels electric. The anticipation I felt was not filled with anxiety but curiosity and joy.

Picture Whoville from *How the Grinch Stole Christmas* during the lead up to Christmas, and that was what the Olympic Village was like all day long. Athletes were skipping around arm-in-arm, hand-in-hand, singing their hearts out as music echoed throughout the Village. It was like I was at an all-inclusive resort. They had around-the-clock service, all-you-can-eat food and drinks, and every night, they threw a massive party.

I tried to enjoy it sparingly. I didn't partake in much of the partying as I was trying to focus all my attention on the task at hand. Debbie had sacrificed so much for me to get here; I would have hated to just party all night and hurt my chances of performing at a top level. I wasn't much of a partier anyway; I'd been a father for four years. It wasn't even a temptation at this point. I was there to make a lasting mark on the sport. I had to do it for myself, and also for Jamie.

First Olympic Fight, vs. Bubagar Samana, August 1984

Bubagar Samana. I found out who my first opponent was going to be hours before the opening ceremonies were to take place. He was from Nigeria, and he was a good first matchup for me. It was during that same conversation I was told that I would be the first Canadian fighter to step into the ring. That's a lot of pressure, and it makes the moment even more nerve-wracking.

I was sweating like a dog at the opening ceremonies. The air was so thick and humid, I couldn't wait to get the ceremony over with so I could go back to my room and focus on my fight. I was worried about making weight, getting a good night's rest and learning as much about my opponent as possible. While everyone was taking photos and enjoying the moment, I was distant and restless.

I woke up extra early the morning of my big fight. There wasn't a scale in my room so I wasn't able to periodically manage my weight the way I'd like to. I hadn't eaten anything for a long time, so I was feeling confident I had maintained my current fighting weight. At eight a.m., I met Hank at the weigh-ins. I jumped on the practice scale, overweight by two pounds. If you're overweight by even 0.1 pounds, you cannot compete.

I had until nine a.m. to shed that extra two pounds, so I threw on my sweat suit and began doing anything and everything to work up a sweat. I went outside in the heat, and for an hour straight, I shadow boxed and skipped. The sweat soaked into my clothing as I felt all the extra water pouring out of my body. I wasn't worried about draining myself for the fight; I just wanted to get to the fight by any means necessary.

I stripped down to nothing, wiped all the water off of my body until I was bone dry and stepped on the official scale. I couldn't look, but Hank patted me on the back, so I knew I had done it. I was half a pound underweight, which meant I was good to go. I had two hours until my fight, which meant I really couldn't eat anything, so all I put back into my body was a Coke and a piece of toast.

The moments leading up to the fight were slow burning. I didn't know what to expect, but I knew I was ready to experience whatever it was I was getting myself into. Much like the Nolan fight, Hank's hands were shaking as he tied up my hand wraps. We're all human. This reminded me of that. We're all human.

My hands felt strong in a pair of brand-new gloves as Hank and I marched down to the ring. Who would have thought five years ago when we started the St. Catharines Boxing Club that we would be in this position? I looked at Hank right before the bell rang and thought to myself, *Here we are*. Right before the match started, we exchanged our countries' flags. This didn't happen any other times throughout the tournament, just during this one fight. And then the bell sounded to signify the start of our match.

I noticed during the first round that he was waiting on me. We both had counter-punching styles, so other than a few faint jabs, nothing was happening. After twenty seconds of that, the ref stopped us and told us to fight. I had never seen that happen before, and it was kind of annoying to have to be told to fight. I didn't panic, though; I just stuck to my game plan and eventually I started opening up my attacks.

I was growing in confidence, but in the back of my mind I was concerned about my legs. I was just hoping that my legs wouldn't tighten up on me after dropping so much water earlier that day. In previous matches where I had to quickly drop weight, I had experienced muscle spasms and Charlie horses. I just kept reminding myself that I was in good shape and hoped for my body to hold up for me.

During the second round break, Hank did what he always did and pulled my shorts away from my stomach to help me breath. His hands were still shaking like crazy. He said all the generic things you'd expect a coach to tell his fighter after an uneventful round, and then he slapped me on the knee and told me to take it to him.

In the second round, Samana came out more aggressive and was also beginning to land his counter-punches. There was a moment early in the round where he caught me with a flurry of four or five punches. He was stealing the round from me, so I knew I had to gain some ground. For the last minute or so of the round, I amped up the pressure and bullied him into the corner. I was confident that I had done enough to potentially steal the round back from him.

I had barely broken a sweat and my legs were feeling really tight as I sat on the stool. Even though I was competing well, I wasn't feeling normal out there. It's almost like I needed two rounds to warm up before I was actually ready to fight. The beginning stage of the third round was when I finally began to get a sweat going. I didn't want to leave anything up to chance so I came out with the mentality that I was going to finish him.

I caught him with an uppercut underneath, an over-hand left followed by a right hook, which buckled his knees. The ref gave him a standing eight count, and I knew he was hurt bad. I landed the exact punch I wanted to land. The uppercut was meant to set him up for the left hand. It caused him to step back, and then he wouldn't see the left hand coming over top.

I knew this was a good opportunity to end the match, so I got right back on top of him and started throwing my best combinations. With a one-two punch, I saw his knees buckle again, and so did the ref. He waved his arms in the air to signify the end of the match. The whole Canadian team was through-the-roof excited. I was more relieved to have gotten my first match under my belt. This was a good win to get Canada rolling. I had a minicelebration within my heart. It settled that I could win fights at the Olympics. I spent the next few days keeping a closer eye on my weight and getting in some light training at the team facility.

My next opponent was Paul Fitzgerald, an Irishman. Hank and I watched his first fight and noticed that he was quite the runner. He'd throw a jab, then back up like five steps. He was always ready to retreat at the first sign of danger. Hank was nervous about this guy and laid out his concerns. I understood where he was coming from, but, if this guy was just retreating the whole time, I knew all I had to do was put my gloves up high and walk him down. The judges would see who the aggressor was, and I should be able to have my way with him.

After Matt Mizerski had seen the draw, he told me before the Olympic competition started, "Steve, if you can get past your first opponent, I can't see a scenario where you don't make it to the finals." The American fighter from my weight class was on the other end of the draw, so I wouldn't have to see him unless we both made the finals.

Second Olympic Fight, vs. Paul Fitzgerald, August 1984

I did exactly what I set out to do in the first round. I put my hands up high, continuously pumping my jab and being the ultimate aggressor. He retreated the entire first round as I attempted to corner him and land my shots. Anytime he threw a punch, it bounced right off my gloves as I held a strong guard up.

140

When I returned to the corner, Hank said, "This guy wants nothing to do with you. Try hitting the body a little more because his head is bobbing around like crazy."

As the fight went on, I got even more aggressive. I was practically running in the ring to keep up with him. I was confident in my conditioning, but I was going to definitely test his. It was super strange to be fighting a guy who was literally running away from me and not landing any punches. I kept him at bay. I would get in close to him, and he had no choice but to throw punches at that point. I would counter him and make him pay in those short moments I had him trapped. It made for a very awkward fight.

I noticed a pattern of movement as the fight went on. He was often circling to my left, so I knew I could set him up for a left hand if I goaded him in. I faked a right hand and got him to circle aggressively to my left where he was met with a telegraphed left hook right on the chin, knocking him right on his ass.

When he got up, Fitzgerald shook his head at the refs and judges as if it didn't hurt him. He was trying to make it look like he slipped. Well, he began running even faster after that. I ran after him, and just kept cornering him against the ropes and pounding on him whenever I could. I had him in a dangerous spot, and the guy grabbed onto my waist and ducked his head below my waist. The ref had to warn him not to duck his head like that.

I chased him down again, and he stuck his head between the ropes. The ref gave the guy another warning and threatened to take a point away next time. I couldn't help but think to myself how weird this fight was. I mean, we're at the Olympics, where the best of the best come to compete, and I was fighting a coward. Near the end of the third round, I caught him directly on the chin, stunning him slightly. For a third time now, Fitzgerald ducked his head between my legs, and the ref stepped in again. He should have taken a point off, but instead, gave Fitzgerald a standing eight count. So with the fight coming to a close, I had forced this guy into two eight counts, and he received two additional warnings.

As the fight came to an end, I knew it wasn't the easiest fight to watch—some may even call it ugly—but I tactically took away any scoring punches he threw. I was the aggressor, and I knew I had won the fight hands down. Hank looked worried as I stood with him in the corner. He told me I won the fight, but he felt like something was off. He was very nervous about the whole situation.

We waited in the center of the ring for literally five minutes for the official decision to come in. I looked toward Hank and nodded at him. I was sure we had this in the bag. I played the fight over in my mind while I stood there, and it felt clear to me that I had won. The ref finally came to the center, grabbed both our hands and the announcement was made. On the video, as the scores are being read, you can see I'm nodding my head along in agreement, while Paul has his head hanging low, shaking his head in disappointment. This was until they announced that Fitzgerald was on the winning side of the decision.

The man was in such shock, that he had to violently turn around and look at what color his corner was to make sure he heard them correctly. I was naturally pissed right off, as this was a complete and utter robbery. I know there are close decisions sometimes, but this fight wasn't even close. Fitzgerald tried to come over to me and raise my hand in the air, and I hated that he did that. All 20,000 attendees in the crowd were loudly booing in disagreement, as they should've been.

I saw Fitzgerald in the back area after the fight with his coach. He said, "Good fight, I think it was close." I looked at him and told him the truth. "I disagree. I won that fight. You better go all the way to the medal round, because if I won I was going all the way." I knew he had little chance. That was the most pathetic fight I had ever been a part of.

Hank tried protesting the fight, but there wasn't really much to go off of. After re-watching the fight and counting the punches landed, I felt even more robbed. For every punch he landed, I landed three. Not to mention I knocked him down once, gave him an additional standing eight count, on top of two warnings. Who knows what the judges were thinking? It definitely felt like I got screwed over.

My heart sank once I realized my Olympic journey was all but over. All I could think about was my family and everybody back home watching, how they must've felt so let down. My closest family cried for me when I lost. Not because I lost, but because of the way I lost. I talked to my dad on the phone, and he said he was proud of the way I handled myself. I didn't stay in L.A. too much longer after my fight. I just wanted to get home. I got on a plane as soon as I could and flew home to my family.

The Pennsylvania Kid

Looking back on my boxing career, one moment sticks out among the rest: It wasn't the Olympics, and it wasn't my rivalry with Nolan. It was actually during a small boxing event in Pennsylvania. It was just at a regular old community center. I would have been around twenty years old at the time. I don't remember who I fought, the exact date or any specific details because it was just another one of those boxing cards we were thrown on to gain experience.

I was slated to fight during the second half of the boxing card. In the meantime, I was sitting in the audience watching some of the earlier fights. Just before intermission, they announced two new fighters about to square off. The interesting thing about the one young guy who came into the ring was that he was really enthusiastic. He looked like he thought he was part of the *Rocky* movies. He had his robe on, he had his hood over his head and he was dancing around like crazy. I thought, *Wow this guy has a lot of energy*. The gentleman who got in the ring across from him looked

144

much older. He had to be about forty-five. I thought, *What a difference in age.* The fight looked particularly different than any other fight I've watched, in the sense that the old guy looked like a regular, skilled fighter, while the kid was very animated. The kid was throwing punches from all different kinds of angles, and the older gentleman had control of the whole situation.

I noticed the rounds were only a minute and a half, as opposed to the three-minute rounds I was accustomed to fighting. So I watched this entire fight and didn't think much of it. But after the fight, that kid was so happy when they announced that he had won the decision. He was smiling from ear to ear and had his hands raised high, dancing all over the place.

Later in the evening, I had a really good fight against a much taller opponent. I won the fight. Then Jamie was in the main event, so I stuck around and watched his fight. After the event, they announced me as the fighter of the night and awarded me a massive trophy, almost as tall as Jamie and I.

I set it up on the table beside me as I was packing up my boxing gear. Jamie came over and was talking to me and admiring the trophy. While we were in conversation, that kid I watched fight earlier came over. He said, "Wow, that's an awesome trophy, man. You fought great. I wish I could've won that trophy. I tried really hard, but you know what, maybe next time I'll get a chance to win something like that. Do you mind if I have a look at it?" I told him to look at it, pick it up—do whatever you want.

So he took a look at it. He was checking out every detail of the trophy. He said, "Thanks a lot. Great fight tonight." I responded, "Thanks, good fight to you too." I kind of watched him walk away because I didn't want to lose track of where he went. So I picked up the trophy, and Jamie asked where I was going. I said, "I'm just going over here for a second."

Jamie said, "I know where you're going."

I followed the kid into a room where he was getting his boxing gear all together. I handed him the trophy. "Hey, look, I think the judges made a mistake. I was watching your fight earlier in the night, and I thought you were really good. You were the best fighter of the evening; I think they made a mistake." His eyes lit up as he said, "You think they made a mistake? Oh man, are you sure?"

I said, "Yeah, here you go. It's yours, it belongs to you."

So he grabbed it and received it, and he said, "Thank you." After that, I left the locker room, and never really thought much of it again. I just wanted to give him the trophy, because I knew he was challenged in some way, and I knew he really loved the trophy.

A couple months later, Hank set up a local boxing card, and called up some American gyms to fill out the card. Some fighters from Pennsylvania were going to make the trip down and participate. I was going to be fighting in the main event that night. Halfway through the fight card, without any notice or explanation,

146

they made an announcement. "Can Steve Pagendam please come up to the ring?" I was like, *What the heck is this all about?* So I made my way to the ring. I saw some men in the ring that I didn't recognize, but they had set up a little display with a boxing ring shaped trophy on it.

The one guy shook my hand and then put the microphone down on the table to speak to me personally. "Son, I want to thank you so much for what you did when you were in Pennsylvania."

I still hadn't really clued in to what he was referring to. He continued, "You gave that young man a trophy. We found him in the locker room, hugging that trophy tightly, just crying. We just wanted to thank you. Our little town has been talking about this Canadian kid that gave his trophy away, and it has been an inspiration to our town."

I had no idea the impact that this gesture was going to make. I just thought it'd be a nice way to make someone's day. The guy in the ring told me that the kid I gave the trophy to, his parents wouldn't even come out to watch him box.

The reason I think I get so emotional talking about this is because if I did anything in boxing at all that I can really say I was proud of, even to this day, that would probably be it.

Welcome Home Steve, 1984

It didn't take me long to get over the sunken feeling that followed the Olympic loss. Once I got home and was embraced by Debbie and the kids, it felt like the biggest bandage had been put over everything that had transpired. This was the end of my relationship with boxing, but life after boxing was poised to be much more rewarding.

I already had a mature perspective on my life, and I knew what was most important. Every decision I made was made with my family in mind. Prior to leaving for the Olympics, I took Debbie for a walk. We walked through all the routes that I had been running for the past six years, going down memory lane. I wanted to take this walk to remind myself of all the sacrifices.

I wanted her to be a part of that moment, because she was a part of this entire journey. Every hill, every trail, every moment of triumph and pain, every second of training—she was part of it. I wouldn't have been able to do any of that without her support and the sacrifices she made. While I was in the gym, she was caring for two little babies, keeping the home together and keeping our family functioning and strong. She handed me a letter and told me to open it after my first fight. Here's what it said:

My Darling Steve,

By the time you get this card you probably should have had at least one fight. I hope you did your best and you're happy with whatever happened. I don't want you to be sad if you lost because you're still the best to me. I've been praying that God will take care of you and not let

148

you get hurt. I sure hope he answered my prayers. I love you Steve and I don't care if you win a gold medal or not. I just hope you fight your best and come home to me still in love with me. You don't need a medal to impress me because you already did that 7 years ago. Win or lose you're my gold medalist in every way that counts. I love you sweetheart. I miss you so much.

All my love, always

Debbie xo xo xo

She will always be my rock forever. I miss you too, Debbie, and love you so much.

CHAPTER IX
Force vs. Flow

The 1984 Summer Olympics

Jamie Pagendam

After the way Steve performed in his first Olympic match, I was very excited to watch him fight the Irishman, Fitzgerald. I knew if he could get through this guy, he was one step closer to winning a medal. The way it was all lining up made it seem like Steve was definitely on his way to the podium. I went to Hank's house to watch the fight with Sherri, but I was unaware that the fight had already taken place and I was watching a replay. Sherri didn't have the heart to tell me what had happened to Steve, so I was oblivious.

I couldn't sit still during the fight, so I stood up and moved as if I were fighting alongside Steve in the ring. I threw punches in the air, cheering with every punch that my brother landed on the Irishman. Steve was chasing him down and cornering him, giving him no room to breathe. When he knocked down Fitzgerald, I jumped around the living room and thought the win was in the bag.

After the match was over, it seemed like an excruciatingly long time to announce the decision.

At the time, I had no doubt in my mind that Steve had easily won the match. When they announced Fitzgerald had won a split decision, the disbelief hit me harder than I had ever been punched. The TV received my verbal wrath, as I yelled and screamed profanities and angry comments toward it. Sherri tried to comfort me and calm me down, but I was very distraught. This wasn't fair to Steve, this wasn't fair to boxing, and it could only be described as downright robbery on the judges' part. All I wanted to do in that moment was be with my brother.

When he returned home, I didn't even know what to say to him. I know he was hearing the same things over and over again. "I'm so sorry. We're so disappointed for you. Are you doing okay?" During a situation like that, what else is there to say? We definitely went over every little aspect of the fight, down to the very finest details. Even after all this, Steve did exactly what he always does; he handled it like a true man. It was nice to see the rush of support and love he got from friends, family and even strangers during the aftermath. It's crazy, but you really see who your true friends are when you get knocked off the mountain top.

To be completely honest, I thought this was the end to our boxing story. I hadn't boxed in many, many months after suffering the cut over my brow. Plus, I knew I wasn't going to be part of the '84 Canadian Olympic team. I still kept in decent shape, but the focus was on getting Steve ready for the Games, so there wasn't much going on at the club during that summer.

I was already contemplating giving up the sport. Seeing what happened to Steve after he worked so hard to get there discouraged me even further. Hank was still pushing me to get back into the gym, and I'd force myself to go and train a little here and there, but it just didn't feel the same as before. The next Olympics weren't going to be for another four long years, and I didn't know if I was ready to start climbing Mount Everest again.

Steve told me that he was ready to just focus on making money and supporting his family, ultimately retiring from boxing. He said that if I was interested he would talk to Matt Mizerski about me taking his spot on the national team. I was definitely interested because that would mean international fights against top-level competitors, which would build up my resume. My dad was excited that I was going to get this opportunity, and he talked to Mizerski about it too.

That was one thing about my dad. Deep down, he was just as competitive as we were, and he took pride in what his sons had accomplished. Dad knew how talented I was at this sport, and he didn't want to see my dreams crumble and go to waste. Remember when he didn't want me to get into boxing? Funny how things can change like that. After Steve and my dad both discussed it with Mizerski, I felt some of my motivation return, and I was ready to give boxing another crack.

I had two weeks or so to get back into fighting shape before the team was to leave for a tournament in Britain. I know all this boxing stuff came naturally to me, but I was jumping onto the national team. These fighters are no joke. As I looked around the plane, I was surrounded by veteran fighters in their mid- to late twenties. You could see the experience they had just by looking into their eyes. Even though I was, again, the youngest among the group, there was a mutual respect right from the get go, and it felt like I was right back in the swing of things.

Since I was taking Steve's spot on the team, I would have to switch to his weight class of featherweight. The chance to be able to follow in his footsteps and have the title of Canadian Featherweight Champion was something I was honored to strive for.

European Tournament, October 1984

My first fight back was against a really tough opponent named Kevin Taylor, who was the British Champion and a southpaw like me. What a way to get right back into the mix. When I was engaging with him, I noticed he didn't have a lot of dynamic movement. For the most part he was pretty flat-footed and didn't move around a whole lot. The one thing I had to be aware of was how powerful his punches felt. Although I was using my footwork to stay out of range, whenever he did pop me, whether it was a landed punch or a block, I could feel his power.

Since he was flat-footed, it made it easier for me to time his attacks with counter-punches. I could tell I was frustrating him, and I felt like the first round went very well despite my lack of training. It took me longer than usual to catch my breath during the round breaks. Taylor Gordon, the coach of the national team, told me in between rounds to keep shaking off the cobwebs. He wanted me to work in some combos and use the next couple rounds to get back into my usual rhythm. Of course, he wanted me to make sure this all was put together in such a way that I still was able to secure a victory.

So when I got out there for round two, I tried to work in my most effective techniques. I wanted to feel like Jamie Pagendam again in the ring. I'm kind of like a shark. When I smell blood in the water, I go for the jugular. I caught Taylor with a right jab to the nose and busted him up, causing blood to spill everywhere. Taylor kept pushing forward despite the blood heavily pouring from his nose. However, I kept having my way with him for the duration of round two.

During the second round break, Gordon had a grin on his face. "You're just as good as Dale Walters," he said. He just compared me to the 1984 bantamweight bronze medal winner. That was all the motivation I needed for round three. I was barely in fighting shape and the national team coach was singing my praises. I thought, *Well, let's go prove what he just said is true.* I found my second gear, and I went into the center of the ring and continued to tee off on Kevin Taylor.

I would parry his attempt and rock him with a stiff jab. I put an exclamation point on the final punch by landing a solid right hook just as the bell was ringing. The crowd jumped to their feet and began chanting, "Canada! Canada! Canada!" Everyone was fired up. My teammates and coaches surrounded me after the victory and were all happy to pump me up. You know what was great about this win? I had no idea I was fighting the British Champion. Nobody told me. I beat the British Champion, and I was only just warming up.

With the European tour over, and in my opinion a great success for me, I was feeling like life was getting back on track. I was back in the gym with Hank, who was fresh off the high of being at the Olympics. He was determined to help me get there too, and there was nothing more important to me than getting to the 1988 Games. Everyone close to me was telling me I had what it took to be the best fighter in Canada. I had people in my ear telling me to start thinking about going pro. Hank had me focused solely on the Olympics though, so I tried to push away all other distractions.

Like I said, everything in my life was falling into place like a well-constructed puzzle. I had good friends back around me, Hank and I were training like animals, and I was feeling close with my family. I was in a good place. I was having fun hanging out with my boys, whether it be playing street hockey, going exploring or, like we did one fantastic day, grabbing some coffee. When I say my life was all coming together like a puzzle, I mean every piece was falling right into the perfect spot, one after another. The final piece of that puzzle greeted my friends and I as we walked into the coffee shop that day. I knew right there, that day, that was the girl I was going to marry.

Meeting Jamie, October 1984

Franny Pagendam

Being brought up by Italian parents, I had always lived in a traditional household. I enjoyed being raised in that environment. It really shaped me into the woman I am today. My parents instilled in me a real knack for creating meaningful, genuine relationships with people. A lot of my personality came naturally to me, so I've always felt comfortable engaging in conversation.

I worked at a donut shop on Merritt Street, and I used to see Jamie drive by in his gold Camaro. The girl I worked with used to say, "Oh, there goes Pag-o." She knew who Jamie was because he was friends with her brother. Her dad and my dad were really great friends, so it was strange that I didn't know who this Jamie guy was.

I saw in the paper that Jamie had just won a medal at a tournament in England. I had never seen his face until I saw it that day in the black-and-white ink of the paper. It just so happened that same day he came into the coffee shop to order something. When he came up to my counter, I asked, "Hey, are you Jamie Pagendam? Congratulations, I heard you won a medal in England." He replied, "Oh, thank you." And that was pretty much it. That was the first time we met.

Jamie had a friend named Dan Rega who used to come around all the time. He became good friends with the girls who worked there, Pam and Phyllis. Another one of our mutual friends who used to work with us was having a baby shower that we were all attending. I guess Jamie had been talking about me to his friend Dan and, when he found out I was going to that shower, he asked Dan if he could tag along with him.

When Jamie walked in, I was really confused as to why he was there. His explanation was that Dan got a flat tire, so he was giving him a ride. It's really funny because, at the shower, I was trying to set up Jamie with my friend Pam the whole night. I had no clue he was interested in me at that point, seeing as though we had only exchanged a limited amount of words with one another.

That same night was my parents' wedding anniversary, so I was planning on heading home early. Jamie insisted he drive me home that night, and I wasn't one to pass up a free ride. I asked, "What about Dan?" Jamie brushed it off and told me not to worry about Dan. It was a long, silent drive back to my house. Jamie reached for my hand, and I wasn't sure what to do so I held his hand, still not saying anything to each other. I really didn't know Jamie, but I was intrigued by the whole situation.

He pulled up along the curb outside my house. I thanked him for the ride, and I went to leave his car. "Wait," Jamie said as he reached out for me. When I turned back toward him, he planted a kiss right on my lips. This had never happened to me before so I was unsure how to react. I just ran into my house as fast as I could. I don't know why I was confused, and I don't know why I ran into the house. My mind and body just started freaking out, and my first reaction was to book it. The next day at the coffee shop, Jamie came in to see me and offer me a ride home from work. I kind of liked him, and I had been thinking about him all day, so I felt comfortable saying yes. After that, I had agreed to see him again and go on an official date. It wasn't long after that I started dating Jamie Pagendam.

We had been seeing each other for around a month when he decided to bring me to his house for the first time. Unbeknownst to either Jamie or I, Jamie's mother Gloria, who had come into the coffee shop on several occasions, had seen me there before and had told Les and many of her friends that I would be perfect for Jamie. So when she met me she started freaking out because I was the girl from the coffee shop!

Australian Games, January 1985

Jamie Pagendam

I didn't have much down time at all. I was either boxing, working or enjoying my new relationship with Franny. Starting this brand new phase of our lives together during a time where I had to be so dedicated to boxing was tough, but she was the perfect type of woman to get us through it. She was strong in every aspect of the word, and the support she showed me never made me feel guilty for one second. She was completely on board with what I was trying to accomplish, and it got to the point where we were going to accomplish this boxing dream together.

Our team was preparing for the Australian Games which was, in some ways, like a mini-Olympics. There were many sports being represented, but Canada was only partaking in the boxing events. I was looking forward to this event because it was going to have an Olympic feel to it.

I had a really great showing in my first match. The Korean fighter I was up against was basically just target practice for me. The shots I was landing on him were quality punches, and this guy just kept eating them like I was feeding him breakfast. The more he pushed forward, the more I punished him. I had to hand it to him, though, he was a tough man. During one exchange I had with him, I misplaced a punch and felt something weird happen to my hand. The most excruciating pain followed, and I began to wonder if I had broken my hand. I toughed it out and won the match despite it all.

Immediately after the fight, I approached the medical team and told them that I felt my hand was broken. Honestly, it felt like they blew me off. They didn't even X-ray me and told me to just throw some ice on it and the swelling would subside. This didn't seem like the type of injury that should be ignored, especially considering that the sport I was competing in required me to use these hands to physically pound on another person.

When it came time to weigh in and forego the medical exam for my second fight, they didn't even check my hands. I mean, I guess it was a good thing, because they wouldn't have let me continue fighting if they found I had a broken hand. We made sure to wrap it up good to help avoid any further damage. It was important for me to finish this tournament because there was one guy everyone was talking about the whole time I was there. He was one of the American's top Olympic hopefuls for 1988, and his name was spreading like wild fire throughout this event. I wanted to face Kelcie Banks in the finals and show him some Canadian love. I mean some Canadian gloves.

My second fight was against a fighter from New Zealand, and even with a tightly wrapped broken hand, I knocked him out in the second round. I was here to win, and a broken hand was not going to dampen my spirits. A broken hand was not going to slow down my momentum. A broken hand was not going to shake my confidence. In fact, I was so confident that, as I was leaving the ring, I noticed Kelcie sitting there, looking a little too comfortable for my liking. I leaned over the ropes and got his attention right away. I stared him directly in the eyes with a giant smile on my face and told him, "You're next."

Sometimes, if you're good enough at it, you can beat an opponent before you even start the match. This type of mental warfare probably wouldn't bother a confident, thick-skinned individual. But if there are cracks in the armor, and you say just the right thing at the right time, you could gain a little mental advantage that could eventually lead to your hand getting raised when it's all said and done. I wouldn't have minded a little bit of a mental advantage, because with that broken hand I was definitely at a physical disadvantage.

From the minute that fight ended against the New Zealander until I had to get in the ring with Kelcie Banks, I had an ice pack constantly in my one hand holding it up against my other swollen hand. I consider myself a tough guy, but damn this was painful. I kept telling myself that I just had one more fight to get through, and then I could let it properly heal. It was time to suck it up and go trade hands with the top American in my weight class.

Even with just one healthy hand, I was able to put together a tremendous effort against Banks in the gold-medal match. Every time I threw my broken hand, I felt a sharp pain course through, what felt like my entire body. I would just bite down on my mouth guard and fight through the troubling pain I was experiencing. I couldn't beat him with just one hand; I had to throw both to stay competitive in the match. Going into the third round, I felt great about the match. Despite the pain, I was winning on every judge's scorecard.

Banks was a great fighter, but I was proving that I was right there with him talent-wise. I was definitely winning this fight without a doubt, but the third round was one of the toughest physical challenges I've ever faced. With every punch I landed with my broken hand, the more the pain increased. It was getting to the point where I almost couldn't handle it anymore. The shock that would jolt through my body was getting more intense with every punch. I blocked a few jabs, and I grimaced harder than I would have if I had taken the shot to the jaw.

I pride myself in being tough as nails, as most fighters do, but it truly got to the point where the pain was so excruciating that I dropped to one knee. It was almost as if my body was screaming at me to stop. I felt like in that moment I had no choice but to stop; I couldn't power through it anymore. My coach knew what was happening and called the fight when he saw me take the knee.

We found out later that there was only twenty seconds left in the third round. I would have won if I made it to the scorecards, but I wasn't even thinking about that. My hand was shattered and raw, and I wanted someone to legitimately look at it and get me on a proper track to heal it. I got the silver medal. I knew deep down in my heart that if I could have finished that match, I would have won gold. But I didn't finish, so to me a loss is a loss. I knew I'd get more opportunities to prove myself among the best. The Olympics were still three and a half years away, and I was thrilled with the high level I was able to compete at so far.

I finally got the doctors to take a serious look at my hand, and they confirmed that it was broken. They set me up in a cast and told me I was going to be out of commission for a little while. I took the recovery time seriously, because a fighter's hands are his money makers, and you can't mess around with that.

While I was sitting at home letting my hand heal up, Kelcie Banks went on to win the World Championships. I was assured that taking time off for my hand wasn't going to disturb my current standing on the national team. The next important boxing event wasn't going to be for a few months, so I could relax my mind and body and just heal.

Healing the Body and Mind, 1985

Although I was itching to get back in the ring, it was refreshing to be able to settle down and spend some much needed time around Fran. We had already created a beautiful foundation, and I was having fun watching us build upon it. Even while my hand was all casted up, I would take her out on the town. At the time I didn't have much money, though, so I had to get creative with some of the dates I took her on. She didn't care either way, as long as we

164

were spending time together. I felt good about where I was heading in boxing, but it's difficult to support a family on a boxer's salary (or lack thereof). I mean, unless you're one of the top guys in professional boxing, it's tough to make ends meet.

Franny, being raised in an Italian household, came from a closely knit, traditional family unit. I knew it wouldn't swing with her father if I tried to marry her while moving up the ranks of the amateur boxing scene. For that reason, I knew I had to get myself a job. Steve proved that you could support a family and work a full-time job while competing for a spot at the Olympics. He made it a possible scenario for anyone trying to achieve their dream. I really wanted to be able to marry Fran, so I did what I had to do.

My dad and grandfather both worked at Fraser Paper Mill, which was a respectable job that would have paid me what I needed to successfully support Fran and I. My main priority was to marry Fran. My dad said if I applied, he could probably get me a job at the mill. So I threw my hat in the ring and, not too long after that, I heard back from their human resources office. They only had available roles for part-time students. I thought, Okay, I'll go apply to Niagara College. I figured if I applied to Niagara College, I would get the admissions office to give me a letter proving my enrollment and bring that back to the mill.

While I was at a training camp in Florida, I got a phone call from my dad. He told me I needed to come home right away because Fraser Paper Mill wanted to interview me in a couple days. Everyone on the boxing team understood that I needed a job, so they sent me home that night.

I came back home, and I went for my interview. I asked the guy during the interview, "What's the possibility of getting hired full-time before the end of the summer?" He went on to explain that there was always a possibility. It was going to depend on how many people retired and stuff like that, but they usually offered those open positions to the students when it was all said and done. I said, "Cool." So, my plan was working. I never had any intentions on going back to school because I hated it. But I got that piece of paper saying I was going to school, and that's all I needed to get my foot in the door.

They had me working at the mill months prior to when my first semester was supposed to start. Every shift I worked, I made an effort to go above and beyond to learn the job. I could tell they were impressed with how quickly I was understanding and grasping everything. It probably helped, too, that my grandfather and dad both had a great reputation at Fraser. It wasn't long before they called me into the office and told me they wanted to hire me for a full-time position. I was ecstatic that my hard work paid off, and even more excited that I didn't have to go back to school.

Senior National Championships, Lethbridge, Alberta, March 1985

My hand felt as good as new, just in time to begin training for the upcoming National Championships in Lethbridge, Alberta. I was keen on winning my second National Championship and, based on my last few performances in the ring, I was primed to do so. Steve hadn't fought since his Olympic upset but was still trying to maintain his place on the team just in case he ever wanted to make a comeback. He was technically on medical leave but was going to come along with me to Alberta for the weigh-ins in order to hold his place on the team.

We took a plane from Toronto International to the airport in Edmonton. Since Lethbridge is such a small town in Alberta, they didn't have an airport that could support big commercial flights. The Ontario boxing team squeezed in this small, twenty-five seat bush plane. It didn't even have a flight attendant.

To be honest, it was kind of fun. The plane was bouncing all over the place like a circus ride. Picture those rickety, old wooden roller coasters, and you'll know what I'm talking about. Steve and I sat at the very back of the plane, so if we ended up going down we could be the first guys to abandon ship out the back door. I remember leaning over and putting my hands over my face, just praying that we survived this flight. It was scary but very memorable.

Since I took Steve's spot as the current Featherweight Senior National Champion on the Canadian team, I held that title. Technically, I had not earned that title yet, but this was my first opportunity to legitimize it. I just had to win three fights, and then I would officially be able to call myself the National Champion.

Let's just say I wanted to make sure this title stayed within the Pagendam family.

The guy I was set to fight first was a fighter Steve had faced before. My brother was able to give me the low-down on this guy's fighting style. The best way to explain what type of fighter Mark Loftus was is by saying he was a smaller version of Mike Tyson. He was someone who would plant themselves solid and look for the knockout with every punch he threw. I was no slouch either. I was known as one of the hardest hitters in the featherweight division at the time.

During my fight against Mark, I took advantage of his strategy to plant himself and made sure I was using my footwork to move around him and stay out of his danger zone. Every time I dodged one of his heavy punches, I landed several damaging blows as a counter. I just continued to punish him with significant blows until I finally finished him off in the second round with a knockout.

I always had success against fighters who had this type of fighting style. This style is effective against slower fighters or fighters who are willing to stand in the center and trade with you; however, against a fighter of my caliber, who excels at counter-punching and effective movement, he would have no chance. My second fight was much different than my first because Michel Moffa was very rangy. He was amazing at timing counter-punches, and our skill sets matched up very closely.

Moffa wouldn't throw any punches until I threw one, and that made it very difficult to land clean shots on him. He was the most difficult competitor I ever had to face, because it wasn't just a fight against the man; it was very much a chess match. Our match went the distance, with me taking a 4-1 decision over Moffa. But man, I had so much respect for that fighter. He really challenged me in the ring and in my mind. He made me a sharper fighter, especially from a mental standpoint.

The victory against Moffa put me in the finals and one win away from being declared Canada's National Champion in this division. The man I'd be up against was Bill Downey. I had never fought Downey before, but this wouldn't be the last time I fought him during my career. Standing at 5'11, he was tall for the division. I had been told he had some real power behind his punches. He was a worthy opponent to be facing in the finals.

As far as I'm concerned, the first two rounds were virtually even. My corner was unsure who had the edge going into the third, but it was believed that whoever had the better third was going to win the match. I looked across to my opponent, sitting on his stool, trying to catch his breath. He was getting tired, and I still felt like I had lots left in the tank. I knew I had the advantage going into the third, and I was going to put on a clinic.

All my training and experience took over, as I walked right through him. I didn't gas out, and it was all thanks to the hours and hours of road work Steve forced into my routine. When the dust had settled, I had done enough to obtain the victory over Downey on a 3-2 split decision. It felt amazing to have captured my second National Championship. My first had been the intermediate championship, so this was my first time winning the championship at the senior level.

I loved being able to boast that I was the top Canadian fighter. It was mostly because I knew how much hard work I had put into boxing that year. Hank was giving me all his free time to train, and he dedicated himself to mentoring me and making sure I had all the resources I needed to reach my goals. I loved winning the championship for him because I knew how proud he was whenever Steve or I won a big match. Speaking of Steve, I was so happy he was there for that weekend of fights. All my family and friends were sending their congratulations for weeks after. I was the National Champion, and it validated all the time I had put into this sport.

A cool part about winning the Canadian championship was that the government now recognized my talents, and I received carded status. That was $450 a month, to help cover my training and travel expenses. That meant I could afford to go fight internationally and build up my resume for the next couple years. I was still working my tail off at the paper mill, but they were very supportive of my boxing. They always accommodated me when I needed some time off to go fight a tournament for the National Boxing Association.

Even though the coaches for the Canadian team were in my corner for national team events, Hank came with me to the North American Championships in Beaumont, Texas. It took time to get used to not having Hank in my corner for important matches, but it felt comforting to have him there supporting me from the crowd.

Hank was in my corner the first time I fought John John Molina in Dominican Republic, and he was going to get the chance to see me take another crack at the #1-ranked fighter in the world at that time. As nice as it was for Hank to make the trip down to Texas, he usually didn't travel this far just to spectate. One thing I remember noticing was how profusely he was sweating on the plane and for the entire trip thereafter. He looked sick, but he insisted he was fine. I couldn't worry about it too much. I had to focus on my fights.

The winner of the Kelcie Banks vs. John John Molina match would face off against me in the gold medal match. I had lost to both of these guys before, but I had a feeling I'd be seeing Banks at some point again down the road. If I could have chosen, I would have faced Molina this time around. Well, as fate had it, my wish came true. Molina would win a tightly contested, unanimous decision over Banks.

The first time I fought Molina, I had dysentery, so this was my chance to prove to him, and myself, that it was in fact the illness that contributed mostly to that defeat. Not to take anything away from Molina, but I know what I'm capable of in there. I knew if I could beat a fighter as well-established as Molina, I'd be making a massive statement to the boxing world.

We both hit each other with our hardest, most ruthless punches, but neither of us waivered. We were trying to eliminate the need for judges by getting a knockout victory. The harder he hit me, the harder I hit back.

Despite all the action in this match, we went the distance, and it was left in the judges' hands. They awarded a 2-1 split decision to Molina. I knew it was going to be difficult to win a decision over Molina, considering where he stood in the rankings. The referee leaned over to me after they announced the decision and told me I fought well, and it very easily could have gone the other way.

I found out later that night that Molina fought through the pain of a badly bruised hand during the tournament. I had to give him credit for that. I know the mental and physical toll a hand injury has on a fighter. I couldn't tell one bit he had a hand injury. He was a true competitor, and we had one heck of an amazing fight that night.

The Canadian boxing manager thought I had won the fight, but he was happy with my performance nonetheless. They put the silver medal around my neck, and I was chosen as one of the two boxers who were going to head to South Korea to fight at the World Cup. Even when I lost matches like this, I still took away the positives. I was becoming a better fighter with every new challenge. Losing to a fighter like Molina still sucked, but it only made me hungrier. My confidence was at an all-time high, and I didn't see anything being able to derail my momentum at this point. That's what I thought, at least.

CHAPTER X
Closed until Further Notice

"If Hank was in my corner at the Olympics, he would have jumped in the ring. I could have won." —*Jamie Pagendam*

September 1985

Hank Boone

Hank held the hand pads for Jamie as the final bell echoed through the St. Catharines Boxing Club, and another day of training came and went. There was as much sweat on Hank's back as there was on any fighter that day. Hank stuck around as, one by one, the fighters left the club to go home for the evening. Jamie was the last to leave that particular night. As Hank often did, he offered him a ride home. "Thanks, Hank, but I'm meeting Fran down the street and we're going to walk home together. Thanks though."

The gym was now empty, and every sound was amplified. Every footstep creaked along the floorboards as Hank walked around the club turning off the lights. The wind outside blew aggressively against the exterior, sounding like waves crashing down on the building.

The club may not have been perfect, but it was his club. What was coming out of the club was all that mattered. Pictures of Steve and Hank at the 1984 Olympics hung on the walls, meant to inspire the up-and-coming fighters to achieve excellence. Steve was just the beginning. Hank was trying to build and sustain a legacy of success for the club—and himself.

Right before he was about to lock up and leave, Hank noticed a pair of boxing shoes lying by the inside of the door. They were white shoes, but he was unsure to whom they belonged. He examined the shoes for a second after picking them up. With the laces of the two shoes tied together, he slung them over his shoulder. In the darkness of the gym, he walked up to the ring in the middle of the house and placed the shoes over the top rope. As they hung there, swaying slightly on the rope, Hank exited his club.

September 7, 1985

Jamie Pagendam

I've had many ups and downs in my career and life in general. Nothing was ever able to completely tear me down because I had the right people around me to lift me back up when I needed it. I was beginning to peak. After losing a split decision to John John Molina, I felt like I was just hitting my stride. I thought, *If we ever get a chance to fight again, I'll make sure I beat him.* Even after losing to Molina, I was going to get an opportunity to represent North America at the World Cup in Korea.

Every big fight from there until the Olympics was a showcase as to why I deserved a spot on the grandest stage of them all. So I couldn't afford to be complacent in my preparation. Even the days I didn't feel like going to the gym, I forced myself because I knew laziness would lead to sloppiness. I grabbed my gym bag, looked for my shoes, grabbed some protein bars and was off and running to the club.

It was one of those overcast days where it felt like it was trying to rain. The air was damp, saturated with rain. Summer was transitioning to autumn, and the leaves would soon become wilted and fall from their trees. The heat of the summer months was morphing into a cool, chilling breeze, which I felt down my spine as I jogged up to the club.

There were no cars outside the club, so luckily I had brought my keys to get in that day. However, when I tried to unlock the door my key wasn't working. I had completely overlooked the piece of paper taped to the door. CLOSED UNTIL FURTHER NOTICE.

My mind didn't go to the worst case scenario; I knew there had to be an explanation. I obviously couldn't train that day, so I jogged back home and began trying to find some answers. I called Hank's house over and over again that afternoon, just hoping to hear the ringing stop and be met with a voice on the other end. It just kept on ringing. I went by his house, but no one was home, and I was concerned. I don't like being left in the dark, so the uncertainty of the situation was making me uneasy. I didn't understand why Hank wouldn't reach out to let me know the club was closed. The fact that he didn't give me a heads up led me to believe that something had happened to him.

It wasn't until later that night that my dad came home and told me what he had seen in the news: Hank had been arrested by the RCMP for drug dealing. My heart sank deep into my stomach, and I became numb.

Hank Boone, 1985–1988

Hank was serving a ten-year sentence for drug trafficking. He had been under investigation for years. Authorities had been monitoring the club, following Hank and watching him closely, but they were never able to get enough to incriminate him. Until Dave Lima came forward, that is.

Dave Lima was a drug dealer who had done some business with Hank. Lima owed Hank, and some other dealers, more than $45,000. After the safety of his wife and children had been threatened, he decided to strike a deal with the RCMP to protect himself and his family. Lima offered to be an informant. In exchange for his help, the RCMP gave Lima and his family $30,000, new names and a new life outside of St. Catharines. The RCMP set up recording devices around Lima's house. During a meeting early in September 1985, Hank and Lima were recorded discussing the sale of a kilogram of cocaine. Hank said he could have it ready by September 6th, and that was the juicy information the RCMP had been waiting for.

Lima was given $75,000 by the RCMP, and the sting operation was a go. Hank arrived on September 6th to make sure Lima actually had all the money before they took separate cars to the drop-off point. Hank made one stop before heading to the exchange. He was supposed to be training with some of the fighters that night, but everything was running a little later than he had previously thought. After a quick drop-in at the club to let the fighters know he would be back soon, he drove to his final destination.

After the drugs and the money were exchanged, Lima got in his car and began driving away. He took off his baseball cap, which was meant to be the signal for the RCMP to swarm the scene and arrest Hank. Time moved slowly as the many squad cars surrounded Hank's car, lifting clouds of dust and dirt in the air.

Although Hank was incarcerated, he was beaming with pride over the fact that Jamie had made the Olympic team in 1988. Even though he had to be more careful with how he spoke in prison, he still made sure lots of people knew about it. On the day of Jamie's fight, Hank made sure to be in front of a television. He was incarcerated at Bath Institution, a low-level security prison just outside of Kingston, Ontario. Hank's hands were shaking as he huddled himself in front of the small TV that they provided for the inmates. With every punch, every movement and every combination, Hank was getting closer and closer to the screen. It was as if he were watching right from the corner like he used to.

Hank knew right away Jamie should have been awarded the win, but there was nothing he could do about it. You could see it in his eyes: He was angry and helpless in this moment. Hank wanted to put his shoe right through the television set. "Jamie had worked his whole damn life for it; you can't put two creampuffs in his corner. I should have been there in his corner."

Autumn 1985

Jamie Pagendam

My heart was broken into pieces. I didn't understand what was happening. I had looked up to this man and trusted him. I put him on a pedestal above my own father. For him to be caught up in that type of business, if that's what you want to call it, was devastating. It emotionally and mentally destroyed me.

The Boones had made me feel like I was part of their family. They treated me like I was their own son. There were years and years of a relationship built, and it all came crumbling down.

Hank was living a double life. Who knows the real reason why he got involved in that stuff. Probably only Hank. But he put us all at risk too.

If there had been any traces of drugs in Hank's car when him and Steve got pulled over at the border, who knows what could have happened to my brother. Steve called him up and talked to him on the phone after finding out what had happened. Steve was pissed off. Being associated with someone like that could have had implications on our lives if we happened to be in the wrong place at the wrong time.

This entire situation really dampened my spirits and caused me to become less focused on my training. When you start getting those anxious feelings in your stomach, all you want to do is curl up on the couch and wait for the next day to come.

I still got myself out to the gym, but I wasn't getting the training that I was accustomed to. Adrian Teodorescu, who coached out of a club in Toronto, offered to pay for my gas if I came and trained at his gym. I ended up going a few times, but the commute was exhausting and draining. I would work a full shift at the mill, then I'd head an hour and a half down the highway to Toronto, then drive all the way back, go to sleep and do it again the next day. It was taxing on my mind and body. My head was just not in the game.

It was a couple months later that Hank reached out to me for the first time since his arrest. He was out on bail and awaiting his trial. Up until then, he'd been keeping a really low profile. He wanted to start going back to the gym to help me train for the 1986 Senior Canadian Championships.

When he reached out, he said, "Hey, I know I messed up, but I still want to help you get to the Canadians, and win the National Championship." I felt a little weird about the whole situation, but at this point I needed some solid training before the championships. He knew how to get the best out of me during training, so I thought it would be beneficial.

Since the St. Catharines Boxing Club was still closed down, we would have to go to the Port Dalhousie Boxing Club and do our workouts. He trained me for eleven days leading up to the championships and, to his credit, he got me in great shape for that amount of time. This was the last time I ever trained with Hank.

Senior Canadian National Championships, Cornwall, Ontario, 1986

Since I was the current champion of Canada, I automatically qualified for this tournament. I asked my dad if he wanted to make it a father-son trip. So we packed up my 1977 gold Camaro, and we headed up to Cornwall. I knew my dad didn't have much money at the time, so I made sure I took care of all his expenses: the hotel, all his meals, everything. I made sure my dad didn't go without anything. However, this all happened after I almost gave my dad multiple heart attacks on the drive up. I was kind of a wild driver as a young man, especially when I was driving a sports car. He did not trust my driving whatsoever, but I just kept bopping along to the tunes and pushing down on the gas pedal.

Obviously, news had spread around the boxing community what had happened with Hank. When I arrived at the tournament, no one would look in my direction. No one said a single word to me. I really did feel like an outcast among my peers, which felt unfair. This made me begin to feel truly bitter toward Hank. You could feel the atmosphere was filled with hushed whispers and sharp judgment. I knew people were talking behind my back. Luckily, I didn't have to depend on any of these people to be successful. Despite all the distractions surrounding me, I looked around and knew I was the most talented fighter there.

To be honest though, I don't know how I would have coped if my dad wasn't there with me. If he didn't come for that tournament, I feel like I would have been discouraged by all the crap going on around me. I wanted to put on some great performances for him and make sure this trip continued to create positive memories. This time with my dad was very important to me because I felt like I wasn't always the best son to him. My dad always had to take a back seat to Hank Boone because I was so enthralled in the lifestyle he was living; I believed anything Hank told me over my dad.

As I looked out into the crowd before my first match, I grinned because I finally felt the appreciation I should have been feeling for my dad this whole time. He had always been out there supporting me during my fights, but this was the first time I allowed myself to truly appreciate it. Even through our rough patches, he was out there supporting from the sidelines, never imposing himself on me. Even when I, to his displeasure, was spending countless days over at the Boones' residence, he would still come out to every boxing event and cheer me on. He was always such a great father, but it took this eye-opening experience to shed light on the truth of the situation.

My first two fights of the tournament were both victories. I made easy work of my opponents and was off to another championship final. This time it would be against Bill Downey. Despite the fact that I had competed in two matches already that weekend, I still felt as fresh as when I first arrived. My dad was boosting my ego, saying this was the best he had ever seen me fight.

Although I would still get myself down a bit when I thought about the Hank stuff, I felt quite relaxed during this tournament. I enjoyed the little moments, like grabbing a bite to eat with my dad in the afternoon or sitting in the hotel room laughing and just chilling. I knew I was going to have to deal with a lot of personal things after the tournament, but, for the time being, I was trying to enjoy the moment.

The fight I had against Bill Downey was one of the best fights I've ever had. He was meant to be a tough challenger for me, but he was walking right into my punches for three straight rounds. He had a few moments during the fight where you could see glimpses of talent, but at the end of the day, I walked right through him to capture my third Canadian Championship.

While I would deem it one of my better performances, there was another reason why I consider it one of my favorite fights: My dad was there at ringside. I looked at him and became very emotional. I rarely got emotional over sentimental things back then, but this felt like a very special moment, and I recognized that.

I felt like this whole weekend really helped my dad and I reconnect and repair our bond. I called my dad up to the side of the ring and I put my gold medal around his neck, pulled him in and told him that I loved him. That was a very emotional time for my dad and I. That was probably the highlight of my entire boxing career, getting to do that for my father.

After a very successful weekend at the National Championships, I was now back at home and, again, dealing with everything. It felt like every day I was faced with different questions, different challenges, and it was really stressing me out. Every time I went to the gym to train, I did it because I felt like I had to. There was no passion in it for me anymore. Everything felt tainted. There wasn't a day that passed by where I wasn't thinking about just quitting boxing and moving on with my life.

I had a good full-time job at the mill; Franny and I were starting to get more serious; boxing began taking a back seat in my life. I hate quitting. It's not something that belongs in my DNA, but those thoughts were creeping in my head, and it scared me. Since it wasn't within me to quit, I remained dedicated and forced myself to focus on my upcoming box-off with Bill Downey. Most days, everything felt half-assed. I was waking up a little later, I was shaving minutes off my workout each time, and I was mentally fatigued.

The human in me was pulling me one way; the competitor in me was pulling me the opposite way. During my last training session before the box-offs, I looked around the gym and took a walk. I was one of the last guys in there as they were shutting off the lights. I just remember the silence. No sounds of fighters hitting pads or the bag, no coaches yelling and no skipping ropes whipping through the air. Just the sounds of a few footsteps and doors closing as another day of training came to an end. I grabbed my bag and my shoes, and I exited the club.

Box-Offs, Cape Breton, Nova Scotia, 1986

The locker room was quiet. I felt like a caged animal. The only thing I could hear was the faint sounds of cheering and, occasionally, a man on a microphone, muffled through the thick cement walls of my cave. I was here because I had to be here. And you could tell that by the way I performed that night.

186

Downey was in his hometown, and the crowd loved every moment of our match. Mostly because Downey was landing on me, and I was having trouble finding my footing. I showed glimpses of pressure, but I was not winning this match. Not a chance. All five judges from Nova Scotia agreed, making it a 5-0 unanimous decision for Bill Downey. I walked back to the locker room with a smile on my face as I passed the massive crowd. I had to smile. It was all I could do to hold back the emotions I was truly feeling. My competitive spirit was gone. Hank stole it away from me.

This was the first time in my life that I've let something distract me to this extent. Even when the coach of the hockey team was trying to derail my hockey aspirations, I set out to prove him wrong. I quit hockey because I liked the fact that boxing was an individual sport, yet, I was allowing my mental focus to veer off because of another person.

My emotions were all over the place. My confidence was dwindling. I didn't understand why this was happening to me. I was treading new waters, and it was making me feel uncomfortable in my own skin. I didn't recognize these feelings that were eating away at me.

I sat in my hotel room and tried not to cry. I just wanted to go home. I felt very vulnerable and embarrassed about how I fought against Downey. Usually that would have motivated me to go in there the next day and punish him, leaving no doubt who the champ was. I would have moments where I could fire myself up back into that mentality, but then my self-doubt would creep right back in.

I had no idea how my next fight with Downey was going to go down. It was already odd that we were having the box-off and the rubber match in the same weekend. I was up most of that night wondering what to do.

Box-Offs, Rubber Match, Cape Breton, Nova Scotia, 1986

I was back in that same quiet locker room. I felt very alone. Usually, I would have Hank there with me. We would hang out and watch some of the other fights, then warm up an hour before my fight. Adrian was working my corner for this weekend, but he was busy with some other tasks he had to accomplish that day.

I heard the door open to the locker room, and it was followed by the echo of many voices. In came eight men, and they were looking for me. They were loyal Downey supporters. They surrounded me as I sat up straighter on the bench. They began to shower me with threats of violence. "You fighting Billy today? Billy's gonna kick your ass." They didn't stop there, saying, "If you beat him, we'll be seeing you out in the parking lot after. All of us." A couple guys threw my stuff across the room and kicked over some stools on the way out.

I sat there in shock. I believed their threats wholeheartedly. This group was not the type to mince words. I was aware of their reputation and was genuinely scared for my well-being. I found Adrian and told him what had happened. I said, "I'm not fighting. This is B.S."

Adrian didn't do anything. He said, "Don't worry about it, Jamie. You're going to win this fight. Don't let them get you off your game."

During the match, I just went through the motions. Normally, I don't pay attention to the crowd, but I could hear everyone during this fight. Everyone outside the ropes was against me, and they wanted to see me fall. I could hear the insults, I could hear the threats; I was so conflicted and unfocused.

Downey caught me with a shot near the end of the round that knocked me down to the canvas. I wasn't badly hurt, but I didn't get up very convincingly. Since it was taking me a while to get up, the ref waved off the fight. I did get up, however, and after looking at me, the ref changed his mind and decided to let me continue, so I was able to finish off the first round.

I was fine; I just took my time getting up. Maybe I wanted the fight to end, maybe I didn't. Taylor Gordon started yelling at the referee after the first round. His argument was that the ref had waved off the fight, so the match should have been over. The ref had to stick with what he had called initially, and they declared Billy the winner of the box-off and the official Canadian National Champion for 1986. I stood at the center of the ring. Everything sounded fuzzy. Everything looked blurry. It wasn't because I was hurt; it was because I was lost. I didn't want to do this anymore. As I walked down the ring steps, I knew in my heart that it was time for me to quit boxing.

Hank Boone Court Hearing, August 24, 1987

"Mr. Boone is a 40-year-old man who has been convicted by a jury of one count of trafficking in cocaine. He has no criminal record," the judge said during the sentence hearing. "He has an enviable record of public service and contribution to the community … While I commend Mr. Boone's public service, I cannot let his proven service to the community blind me to the destruction caused to the community by the distribution of a dangerous, hard drug like cocaine."

Hank sat there with his lawyers as the judge addressed him and the courtroom. He had gained a lot of weight, so his suit barely fit him. It was a mix of stress eating and a rare kidney disease called focal segmental glomerulosclerosis (FSGS). He was sweating from the nerves of not knowing what his future held.

"Would you please rise, Mr. Boone?" asked the judge. "Do you have anything to say to the court?"

"Yes, Your Honor. I've—I lived a clean life until I met Mr. Lima. That's pretty well all I've got to say."

"Henry Arnold Boone, I sentence you to a period of incarceration of 10 years."

The newspaper report at the time of his sentencing said things like he had led a "double life," or that people didn't know the true Hank. It also said he showed no remorse but smiled as he left the courtroom on August 24th.

"Nobody in the world could have been more depressed than me," said Hank, speaking from Bath Institution about smiling in the courtroom. "It was all I could do to stop from crying."

The man loved boxing, but trying to keep his club open was his knockout. Hank served his ten years in prison. His passion for boxing never faded. He was even training some inmates during his stay at the Joyceville Prison. When he got out of prison, it wasn't long before he was holding hand pads for the next generation of boxers at the club.

CHAPTER XI
Road to Revival

1987

My feet were resting up on the porch as I leaned back in my chair, cracked open an ice cold beer and watched the sunset with Franny. The breeze I felt along my neck raised the hairs on my arms, but they quickly settled back down as Fran cuddled up with her warm touch. We had the day off from work, and there was nothing distracting us from just being together. For the first time in a while, my mind had slowed right down, as if it were approaching a yellow light. My foot may have been pushing down on the brake, but my relationship with Fran was pedal to the metal. I never wanted to leave these moments because they were filled with pure love and joy. As the sun set and the breeze became increasingly more chilly, I grabbed the thick blanket to my left, wrapped us up tightly and continued to cozy up with my woman. Life was quiet, and it was the happiest I had ever been.

It was nice to step back from boxing and see what else life had to offer. Since the age of eleven, it had been pretty much nonstop for me. I had to put a lot of things in my rear view mirror and just keep driving. I couldn't participate in any other activities I enjoyed because of the time I needed to dedicate to boxing. You know how many exciting and fun events I missed out on with friends because of my strenuous schedule? My pursuit for a special spot in boxing history was time-consuming and demanded my full attention.

Although I eventually got myself into a place where I could enjoy life, it was a difficult transition for me early on. I ate, drank and slept boxing for the better part of my youth. In a way, it was all I knew. Unfortunately, the circumstances that were dealt to me left me with a bad hand and I folded. It's not that my heart wasn't into boxing, it's that my head wasn't. The stress was getting to me, and it was making me unhappy and changing me in ways I didn't like. With everything that had happened the year before, I couldn't focus the way I needed to. I chose to pursue boxing because I fell head over heels in love with the sport. If I was just boxing because the Olympics were coming up and felt like I had to stick it out, then it was already a losing battle.

Too many things had changed: I lost my coach and mentor in a challenging way, and Steve hadn't boxed in three years; I was trusting my preparation with people I didn't know very well. For the first time, I had really started doubting myself. Thoughts crept into my head and began planting seeds. The doubt didn't just extend specifically to boxing related issues; it was leaking into my everyday life. A part of me wonders if it was due to the fact that I was making such drastic life changes.

It's easy to blame the circumstances, but people have gone through tougher obstacles and still fulfilled their dreams. When you compete in combat sports, you have to have that ambition inside of you. If a lion's not hungry, it won't chase down its prey as aggressively. My hunger was gone, and my head was not in the proper mindset for this type of commitment. My moment in the spotlight was up, and it was time to move on to bigger and better things.

The Proposal

Franny Pagendam

Jamie and I were looking at different engagement rings at the Pen Centre shopping mall one day, and I was making comments on ones I thought were pretty and ones I thought were not so pretty. I was making fun of this one ring in particular. I said, "Oh look, a Mrs. Chancellor ring," like the character from the soap opera *The Young and the Restless*. On the show, she always wore rings with really big diamonds. Well, of course, that's the ring he had bought for me weeks earlier. I was only joking; it was a very, very beautiful ring.

We went out for dinner at Mister C's that night, and just by the way everyone was acting, I could tell something was going on.

The entire evening was really great, and Jamie and I had a very nice time. He didn't propose at the dinner, though. It wasn't until we got back home that he got down on one knee and asked me to marry him. At first, I said no in a shocked reaction. He looked at me strange, and then I smiled and said yes, of course.

I'm thinking I said no, as my initial reaction, because I was probably mad at him about something he did. Back then I was always getting frustrated at him because he could be very foolish. Not foolish in a bad way, but foolish in the way all young men can be foolish. But we were so happy together, and I couldn't believe I was engaged. We eventually got married on November 28th, 1987.

Fraser Paper Mill, April 16, 1987

Jamie Pagendam

I found a nice home for Fran and myself, with a big yard; it even had an in-ground pool. Back then, it cost $52,000, which was affordable for us at the time. They wanted a decent down payment, which would have been difficult to meet if I didn't end up selling my beautiful red corvette. So I said goodbye to the coolest car I had ever owned and made the responsible choice for my new family.

Similar to when I was boxing, I was starting to get into a routine. Obviously, I had my weekly work schedule, which was your standard shift work. After work, I'd get home and have dinner with Fran, and then we'd spend time together until it was time to hit the hay. It was a simple, cliché routine, but it was all good with me. It was stress free and, for the first time in months, I had a genuine smile across my face.

I loved waking up on a beautiful spring morning and having breakfast and coffee at the dining room table. I'd walk outside and enjoy feeling the warm, rising sun meet me in the driveway. I'd get in my vehicle, drive to work, get there ten minutes early, punch in and do my duties for the day. I was set in my ways, and it gave my life fluidity and harmony. I was a working-class citizen, and I found great pride in providing for my family. I appreciated my simple routine. I mean, sure, there were days I'd be running a little late or days where it would be raining, but when your routine gets broken up a little bit, usually it doesn't affect your life too much. But then there was the day I drove to work, got there ten minutes early and the building was blocked off and surrounded by ambulances. This was a life-altering shift to my routine.

I was scheduled to work that day, but as I got closer to the scene, I knew that wouldn't be the case. Written all over the faces of the people surrounding the building was turmoil. Some people had tears in their eyes as they tried to collect their emotions. Only certain people were allowed to go inside at this point, so I didn't see the physical scene.

I came across many people who didn't have any answers, and many others who only had small details to share. But through it all I found out that one of my co-workers, Darren Tucker, had been in a serious, life-threatening accident. A 1,500-ton bale of paper rolled onto him while he was operating the tow motor. My heart sank learning this information. As a young man, I began processing a lot of different emotions. I had never been around such a physically traumatic event before, and it really puts things in perspective fast.

I didn't know Darren well, but I knew him enough to say hello and wave if we ever crossed paths in the mill. He was a co-worker but, no matter the depth of my relationship with him, it is always scary and concerning when something devastating like this happens so close to home. This could have happened to anyone, including me, and I can't imagine how Darren and his family were feeling that day and in the weeks and months following.

Darren survived the accident but was paralyzed from the neck down permanently. The plant was shut down for a couple days to give everyone some time to process the situation. I naturally felt awful for the family. I called my dad and talked to him on the phone about it. I talked to Fran about it, but this was really sticking with me. He was constantly in my thoughts, and I just couldn't move on from it. I really wanted to do something to help, but I kept thinking to myself, *What could I possibly do? I'm just a young guy at a paper mill.*

My dad joined the committee in charge of finding ways to raise money for the Tucker family to cover medical needs and any future costs that may come up. My dad used his marketing skills to set up successful fundraising events such as pledge drives, BBQs and dances. Over a ten-month period, they had raised a lot of money for Darren and his family.

It wasn't long after that my dad approached Steve and me about headlining a boxing event to hopefully reach the financial goal they had set out to raise for the Tuckers. I was at least thirty-five pounds overweight, hadn't worked out in months, but it was a no brainer. Of course I had to do something to help him. This was an obligation that I had to fulfill, and I was happy I was getting a chance to help out the family.

Even though it was a boxing event to raise money, it was still a fight. I had to get back into fighting shape if I was going to agree to do this. I'd still be fighting in front of an audience of people, so I wanted to fight earnestly. I returned to the gym and was training the same way I did before I left the sport. If people were going to pay to come see me, I was going to give them a performance to remember.

My body was used to being at 126 pounds, so it didn't take too long to lose the weight. My favorite part of the whole experience was getting to be back in the gym with Steve after more than three years. That gave me the extra spark I needed and made training enjoyable for the first time in a while.

Putting on the gloves and the headpieces, getting in the ring to spar with my big brother was slowly reminding me of why I fell in love with the sport in the first place. It was something Steve and I had built together. We discovered it together. We became passionate about it together. We won together, and we faced our losses together. I couldn't help but smile as we circled around the ring for the first time, throwing a couple faint jabs. It brought me right back to the very first times we sparred against each other.

I would wake up at five a.m., kiss Fran on the head and run to the gym. Before, going to the gym was just part of my routine; now I was excited to get out of bed and hit the gym. Since Steve and I both worked shift work, we didn't train together every day, but we both found our own times to get in the work we needed. Since there was no more St. Catharines Boxing Club, we were training out of Merritton Boxing Club. It was a newly established gym run by Joe Corrigan.

I had slimmed down to my fighting weight and was back to looking like Jamie the fighter. Fran was excited to see me get back in the ring one more time, and she could see how excited I was as well. I was catching the boxing bug again. As much as I enjoyed being back in the mix, I continued to remind myself that this was it for me. I was happy with how my life was going, and I didn't want to screw any of that up. I was fighting to help the Tucker family and to end my career on a good note.

Darren Tucker Benefit, Merritton Community Centre, February

1988

I was nervous the night of the benefit. Not scared nervous, but the kind of nervous you get when you're about to showcase yourself on a stage. It could be anything in life. An artist revealing a painting they've been working on for a while, meeting your significant other's parents for the first time, a musician performing a new song or a boxer coming out of retirement to show he still has some gas left in the tank. When you're sharing something with the public, it's a different kind of vulnerability. I enjoyed the pressure of the moment, though.

Some of my nerves came from uncertainty. The last string of fights I had before I hung up the gloves were poor performances. I had lost my confidence and my will to fight after the Downey match. What if I went in there and embarrassed myself in front of this local crowd? These were thoughts I'd never had to deal with before. I was already a confident fighter on my own, but I had a coach who constantly was giving me positive feedback and overwhelming praise. I stood off to the side and tried to relax as my brother Steve was making his way to the ring for his match.

Steve fought before me, and it was like he turned back the clocks. I felt like we had been transported back to 1983. Steve hadn't boxed in four years, but he looked just as mesmerizing as the times he fought against Nolan. My nerves started to subside a bit as I watched Steve confidently walk down his opponent and hit him with some nasty combinations. The match ended with Steve winning by unanimous decision.

After his fight, I walked into the back area to get ready for my match. I had already warmed up; I just needed to get myself mentally prepared. I was moments away from entering what used to be my domain. A domain that I never thought I'd be in again, but there I was. I listened as they announced my opponent, Scott Versterfelt, to a humble applause from the 600 fans seated around the ring. All the familiar feelings of adrenaline and excitement coursed through my body as I anticipated my entrance. I didn't know what to expect from the fans as I walked through the open door, but I was hit with a thunderous ovation. Everyone jumped to their feet, and it really had me taken aback.

Even though so much was going on, I saw all the familiar faces as I made my way to the ring. My parents were proudly cheering as their son bounced along toward the ring. I saw Fran and Debbie in the stands clapping, followed by one of Franny's famously loud whistles. I saw Darren Tucker and his family, and I realized how important a moment this was. It wasn't about me. Look at how many people showed up to support the cause. It was already a win for the Tucker family and our community.

The bell rang and, just like Steve was able to turn back the clock, I too did not miss a beat. I just kept smacking him, using my entire arsenal, and eventually in the first round, I was able to stop him. The crowd went wild, and it felt like it went on forever. They honored me with the Barber Memorial Award for fight of the night. I knew what I wanted to do with it immediately. I walked over to where Darren was sitting and I gave him the award, because no matter how hard any of us fought that night in the ring, it was not even close to how hard this man had been fighting for his life.

Mr. and Mrs. Tucker were so overwhelmed by what my dad and all the other members of the community did for their family. I was so blessed to be part of it. It is still, to this day, the most important thing I ever did in my boxing career. The benefit ended up raising $45,000 for the Tucker family.

The benefit gained a lot of attention from Canadian boxing officials when my name was attached to it. I had way more experience than any other fighter they had in my weight class, and with the Olympics coming up, they all came out to see if I still had "it." They hounded me after the match, trying to get me to make an official comeback and an attempt at making the Olympic team.

I had planned on just coming back for the one fight, like I said, but I felt like I got my swagger back, and it boosted my ego having all these national team representatives approaching me. It was tempting, but I didn't want to rush into any decisions.

I remembered how I felt sitting on the porch. I knew if I decided to jump back into the world of boxing, I'd have to put those special, intimate memories I was creating with Franny on hold for the time being. I had to really weigh the pros and cons. On one hand, I know how stressed out and anxious I was feeling at the tail end of my last boxing stint. Like I said, the hunger was gone and I felt like I was forcing myself to keep going. I thought, *What if I commit my time back to boxing and I fall back into the same complacent mindset?* On the other hand, my stomach was empty, rumbling, and I was hungry again. Being back in the ring and having a purposeful match renewed the ambition inside of me. I was still unsure.

It was Vinnie Ryan who got under my skin, saying something along the lines of "Jeez, Jamie, you should be going to the Olympic Games. You're too good to let your talent waste." He came from the McGrory's Boxing Club in Hamilton. He wanted me in his gym, so he got the ball rolling for me. I said, "Well, if you can make it happen, make it happen." It was really encouraging to see how invested the Canadian coaches were to getting me back in the ring.

I didn't want to make this decision alone. I really didn't want to be selfish either. Fran and I were a team now, so this big decision was going to be made together. I seemed to be the one lingering on the cons. Fran stopped me in my tracks. She could see it in my eyes that I needed to get back between the ropes. She told me the porch wasn't going anywhere any time soon. That's all I needed to hear.

The Provincials had already taken place. Therefore, what needed to be set up was a box-off with the current Provincial Champion. This would have to be something the current champion agreed to, as he had no obligation to put his title on the line heading into the Nationals. Of course, he refused to do so. If I didn't have a spot at Nationals, then there would be no chance at the Olympics.

Although I didn't catch a lot of breaks during my career, I had a few fortunate moments come my way. The current Provincial Champion left the Ontario team and decided to turn pro, which opened up a spot for me. Vinnie was able to get me back my spot on Team Ontario to compete at Nationals. This was such a convenient set of circumstances for me, but I knew I still had to take advantage of this golden opportunity.

Vinnie was kind of like a Hank. Vinnie wouldn't do any of the training, but he wanted to build up his gym. To be completely candid, a lot of the coaches who run the clubs don't do a lot of the actual coaching and training. Many of them haven't even boxed before. When it comes to the national team, it becomes more political than sport. It is what it is though.

At the end of the day, I had to make a decision. All the coaches knew I had a great shot at making the Olympics, so they wanted me to join their clubs. I was a political pawn. It was all to get votes to see who would be one of the Olympic coaches. The more fighters you had, the more votes you'd get. Adrian

Teodorescu, who had Lennox Lewis training out of his gym, was really trying to get me to join his club in Toronto. I always liked Adrian but, with my job, I didn't want to have to travel too far away from home.

I had many talks with Vinnie and Val Ryan and, although I appreciate the work Vinnie had done for me, including his great support, I just felt I needed a more established, veteran coach. Plus, again, Hamilton was quite the hike for training. I had been training out of Merritton Boxing Club, during my preparation for the Tuckers' boxing benefit. Joe Corrigan is a great coach, but I just knew I needed that something more to give me the edge.

Ray Napper started getting into my ear, "If you go to Toronto, there's a possibility you might not go to the Olympics." The thing about Ray was that he was well-respected and well-liked by the boxing community, so the national team would have loved to name him as a coach. If I went with Adrian, he would have had more votes than Napper. If I joined Napper's club, he would be tied with Adrian, and they would take Ray over Adrian because of his reputation.

After having a heart-to-heart conversation with Ray about boxing and family, I decided it was the right fit for me. It was close to home, being in Welland, and Napper was familiar with the Pagendam brothers, so I knew I'd be well respected. The other Olympic hopeful from this club was Tom Gilesby. He was a tough kid. I was really excited about my choice and, now that I had a solid club to train out of, I was ready to get myself prepared for the months ahead.

Canadian Championships, Edmonton, Alberta, March 1988

This entire comeback would be derailed quickly if I didn't end up winning the Canadian Championship. I knew I'd get a chance at a box-off, but I needed to get some wins under my belt to show the national team who they were dealing with.

I was against the tallest opponent I had ever faced, Kellie Crowell. My focus for the fight was to nail him in the body with bruising hooks and then eventually clock him in the head. The first round, I executed phase one of my strategy. I just relentlessly pounded his body, wearing him down and breaking his spirit. In the second round, I continued to work the body before eventually delivering a combination of nasty blows to the head, dropping Crowell to the canvas on two occasions, before I put him out of his misery with a third and final knockdown.

I definitely had my mojo back in that performance and, in doing so, recaptured my title as Canadian Champion. This was only the first stage of the Olympic qualifiers, but I was ecstatic. I knew this was going to be a journey so I had decided to just enjoy the ride.

All I had to do was defend my title in a box-off against Wesley Sunshine (what a great name), and I would officially be the National Champion for 1988. If this guy somehow beat me, I'd have to fight him again, like when Steve fought Nolan three times. I didn't want it to come to that; I just wanted to win this fight and then focus my energy on solidifying my spot on the Olympic squad.

I didn't want to take any risks. This was my moment, and I wasn't going to let Sunshine creep in and take it away. I picked him apart using my experience and speed for three rounds and rode that performance to a unanimous decision. Even after sinking my teeth into the National Championship, I wasn't guaranteed a spot on the team. I'd been away from boxing for almost a year. I wasn't quite ranked where I needed to be. There was some work left to be done in order to jump into the top sixteen in the world.

Canada Cup Tournament, Ottawa, Ontario, June 1988

The best way to work your way up the rankings was to win some international bouts against solid competitors. The national team headed down to Ottawa for the Canada Cup, which saw thirty-plus countries competing. The main purpose of this tournament was to give national team boxers the chance to improve or earn rankings on the world level. This was exactly what I needed, but I needed to show up or I could kiss my Olympic dream goodbye.

I hadn't fought so much in a short amount of time since Hank was setting up my matches. The tough part was that in this short time, I would be fighting three to four quality fighters.

My first fight was against a Russian fighter named Abdibahit Khalmurzayev. Just by how he came out of the gates, I could tell he was a top-notch fighter. He boxed well and he moved well. Once I started to adapt to his style, I caught him twice halfway through the fight. He was given two standing eight counts. Late in the fight, Khalmurzayev laid a gruesome blow to the back of my kidneys, which effectively knocked the wind out of me and dropped me to a knee. I received a standing eight count, but I was able to regroup and come away with a unanimous decision victory. I don't know if you've ever been hit in the kidneys, but it hurts like hell.

The next day, I fought Rodney Garnet, an American fighter. I was able to outbox him too, racking up my second victory of the tournament. The soreness in my kidney area was starting to bug me a little bit. It was an annoying, nagging tightness around my lower back. It kept getting tighter and tighter as I fought through four consecutive days of fights. I would end up losing my final fight of the tournament to David Anderson, a Scotsman. It was a close match, but he edged me out in points.

My performance in the Canada Cup was as good as I could have hoped. I was able to defeat three out of the four men I faced. But, despite my success, my spot on the Olympic team was still up in the air. I always thought deep down that I would be going. By then, it was almost August and the Games were in September, and I was thinking to myself, *Holy crap, I might not be going.* My work was sponsoring me, paying my wages while I took time off to train, and I might not even be going. It was stressful.

The committee was still reviewing my situation. For the time being, they tentatively had me scratched in on the team while they gathered further information. All the other members of the team had been officially named already. All I could do was continue to work hard, train hard and really just pray for the best. I didn't know what was going to happen, but I didn't feel comfortable where I was sitting.

I'm not the kind of guy that likes to leave things to chance. I'm also not the kind of guy who likes to leave things in other people's hands. I will always bet on myself, and if that means taking a risk to ensure that I get what I want, you best believe I'll jump on that opportunity.

While the national team was having a training camp in Ottawa, during and after the Canada Cup, Ray Napper approached me. They were setting up a pre-Olympic tune-up which would be aired on NBC between Canada's top fighters and America's top fighters. I was asked if I wanted to be part of that card. Of course I did, and I had an even better idea.

I took Ken Napper, the team manager for the Olympic team, aside and said, "Look, I haven't been named to the team yet. So if I'm fighting an American, I want to go against their world champion, Kelcie Banks." Napper agreed and set it up. If I could beat Banks, on American soil, I knew it would solidify my spot on the Olympic team.

CHAPTER XII
My Partner: Pain

August 1988

I demanded a fight against Kelcie Banks. I felt that if I proved myself against a proven champion, and an American Champion no less, they would have no choice but to send me to the Olympics. I was forward-thinking, and I took a risk. If I had fought any other fighter on that card, there was a good chance, win or lose, that I wouldn't be chosen for the Games. So I was going to fight the World Champion, and I was going to bull right through him on NBC so everyone could watch.

Even if my hand broke this time around, I was going to smash him with it. Even if my hand dislocated from my wrist, I'd swing it around and try to hit him with it. I was winning the first time we fought, but the pain forced me to quit. I won't let that happen ever again, especially not on the road to the Olympics. Pain would be my partner from this moment forward.

I was listening to some music and trying to visualize the way I wanted the fight to go. As I was doing this, I heard a very familiar voice in the distance. I was able to tune everything else out for that moment and listen. I turned around to an amazing surprise.

My parents and Franny had made the trip down to North Carolina to watch my fight against Kelcie. I didn't need any extra motivation for this fight, but I definitely got it when I saw their faces.

After I weighed in the morning of the Banks fight, I took Franny on a little sightseeing adventure. It was nice that we got to spend time together because if I were to make the Olympic team, I wouldn't see her for almost a month. The Olympic team was headed straight to a two-week camp after this fight card, and then right to the Games in Korea after that.

While we were enjoying ourselves I did something that afternoon that I had never done before: I tried to carbo-load in order to gain some extra strength. That's not the reason I did it, but I didn't think it would hurt me. I justified it by saying it would give me extra strength, but in reality I just wanted to enjoy myself. I indulged in some pizza, some plates of pasta and even had an ice cream cone for dessert. I mean, it was four or five hours before my fight, so I didn't think it would affect me in a negative way. I've eaten foods like this prior to fights before. I've always been able to digest properly, especially with this much time in hand.

Canada vs U.S.A. Olympic Tune-ups on NBC, August 1988
I was becoming a tiny bit concerned right before I walked out for the fight because the food I ate hadn't digested completely yet. I felt myself carrying it around in my stomach, and I felt sluggish. I

still felt very bloated from all the treats, and it affected my performance in the early phases of the fight.

If I had maintained a proper fighter's diet like I normally did, I could have been even faster and stronger, and I would have had more energy. As I settled in to the first round, I began feeling better and more like myself. I just hated feeling the food sitting in the pit of my stomach. Despite the sluggish start, I still felt like I was performing well and executing my game plan. Like I said, pain was my partner. I did not want to make any excuses. If I felt bloated, then I was just going to have to fight through it and win bloated. Luckily, I didn't have to worry too much about it, everything felt back to normal after the first round.

This would have been a tough fight to score for the judges. All the rounds were pretty close. Steve says he thinks I won every round of the fight and, watching it back, you can definitely make that case. However, it would have been tough to score because Kelcie was throwing a lot of punches.

Although he was throwing many punches, a lot of them were landing on my arms and elbows. It was just pitter-patter. I was slipping his punches, blocking his shots; my defense was really on-point that night. When he came in close, I had my hands up protecting myself completely. I may have not thrown as many punches as him, but every punch I landed was clean. My punches were snapping his head back consistently, but my head never snapped back, not once. He touched me during the fight, for sure, but didn't do any real damage.

As for the American crowd, you could slowly feel their support shifting toward me. Any time I caught Kelcie with a good shot, you could hear a little roar from the crowd, signifying excitement. When I say that, I don't mean the whole crowd was backing me, but the tone was definitely different than how it was from the onset.

Jamie Pagendam vs. Kelcie Banks

Franny Pagendam

I was sitting in the stands watching the fight with Jamie's parents, and there was a guy in the crowd behind us really irritating me. He was aggressively booing every Canadian fighter, making obnoxious remarks about the country. During Jamie's fight, I had had enough, and I turned around and started a fight with him.

I told him he was being a giant idiot and to shut his mouth. We engaged in a back-and-forth of insults and threats. When the man stood up, Jamie's dad stepped in and tried to diffuse the situation by telling the guy, "That's not what she meant." I piped up after that and said, "No, that's exactly what I meant!" Some of the places we would go and watch Jamie fight would get pretty hostile, but I always remember this one exchange very clearly.

Jamie Pagendam vs. Kelcie Banks

Jamie Pagendam

In the second round, I sealed the victory in my mind when I knocked Kelcie down with a perfectly placed right hook. I landed it right across his chin, and he dropped to the canvas. I knew right then and there that I had the fight. When I played the fight over in my head, I couldn't see any other outcome but a victory.

When the decision was announced, the crowd was displeased. I'll never forget their reaction. Kelcie Banks had won a 2-1 split decision. The television commentator described the American crowd's reaction, pointing out that the crowd disagreed with the judge's decision with "overwhelming boos." I obviously agreed with the crowd. Clearly, the judges must have been watching a different fight than the fans.

The American crowd booed against their own fighter because they believed strongly that I had won the fight. Ken Napper was pissed after the fight, saying, "It was a disgrace. I was ashamed that our own Canadian official would vote against us. It was uncalled for. Pagendam clearly won the fight."

There were three judges: an American, a Canadian, and a Mexican. The American voted for Kelcie (obviously), the Mexican chose me as the winner, and the Canadian judge saw Kelcie as the winner. I was disappointed because I would have expected our native judge to back our athlete in a close fight. I'm sure the

American judge was a little biased, but then I would expect the Canadian might have been biased as well.

Later on that day, I was sitting near Kelcie Banks. He came over to me, and we chatted for a short while. Kelcie told me that he felt I had won that fight, and I appreciated him saying that. I felt like I had earned the victory as well. He said, "Well, I guess I'll see you in Seoul." Banks walked away after, but I was still unsure if I was actually going to be seeing him in Seoul. I still had not been named to the team officially.

It wasn't until much later that night that Ken Napper took me aside, while we were still in North Carolina, and informed me that I was now officially on the Olympic team heading to Korea. Everyone was impressed with my performance against Kelcie, despite the judge's decision.

After I found out I was officially an Olympian, I noticed my training became more fluid. I wasn't training under stress anymore. Being told I was on the team lifted a weight off my shoulders and set me free. Having fought at the Canada Cup and then against Kelcie, I was already in phenomenal fighting shape. Going to my corners between rounds, I was barely breathing hard. My road work and in-gym training was paying huge dividends.

Olympic Training Camp, Burnaby, B.C., August 1988

Prior to the Olympics, the team met up in B.C. for two weeks to get some focused training in. Every morning, we would wake up and run 10 kilometers, and I would make sure I won that run every time. It wasn't a race, but I wasn't going to jog next to a buddy and talk; I was there to get myself ready. My thought process was that if I beat all these guys, then I was better than them. It helped with my mental preparation. I'm happy I was disciplined enough to push myself, because I wasn't going to receive much help at the Olympic training camp.

Even being part of the Olympic team, I was still overlooked and pushed aside. They didn't have any sparring for me. The coaches wouldn't let me spar the bantamweights, or any of the other featherweights; they had me sparring welterweights. Welterweights were three weight classes above mine. For those who don't know, that's a twenty-pound difference.

The reasoning behind it was because the welterweights would potentially face some tough southpaws at the Games. So they used me for sparring, even though I'm on the team, to help the other fighters prepare for their Olympics. No one was preparing me. I had to prepare myself, which pissed me off.

If you're not getting good sparring rounds in, then you just have to shadow box harder, hit the bag harder and do as much individual training as possible. I had been in the ring enough; I knew what it felt like to be engaged in a match. I just pushed myself during all the other stuff and knew I had the mental stability to feel ready without proper sparring.

You know what else? None of the coaches did any pad work with me during those two weeks. Not once. It was one of the worst training camps I had ever been a part of. It seemed like the coaches were just there to get their Olympic rings. Steve had a similar training camp experience. He told me his Olympic training camp was pretty awful too. I was not there to make excuses, though. I just kept my nose to the grindstone and got myself in the best shape I could.

After I got through the two weeks in Burnaby, I was ready to go to Seoul. The team had bonded nicely together, so I was looking forward to the trip. I knew I had a real, legitimate shot at winning a medal. I didn't care who else believed that because I knew inside my heart that it was true.

Seoul, Korea, Ten Days Prior to the Olympics, September 1988

Reality set in for me when we were on the plane. I had my Olympic-themed sweats on, I was with my teammates, and the pilot made an announcement acknowledging the boxing team was on the flight. This is when it felt most real because there was no turning back now. We arrived ten days before the opening ceremonies so we could get used to the environment. I definitely wanted to get settled in, but before I could do that I had to get my souvenir shopping out of the way. This also gave me a chance to see a bit of the city.

The layout of their city was much different than ours. For one, I did not see a single house: It was all apartment buildings or complexes. With no traffic lights at any intersection, the roads were a free-for-all. All you can do is trust the cab driver at that point. It felt good to get my souvenir shopping out of the way. I dropped close to a thousand dollars on that first day, but now I could solely focus on the task at hand.

The Olympic Village was really cool and exceeded my expectations. All the athletes were so jubilant and positive. The environment was very uplifting. Everyone there was willing to talk and embrace the moment, and it created a powerful sense of comradery. They had the boxing team stay in the same complex. Some of the guys were very relaxed and focused, while others were on edge and anxious. I think everyone was eager to get back to work. I gave myself a day to settle in and enjoy the festivities, but then it was time to get engaged.

I had some work to do, seeing as though I was currently eleven pounds overweight. That wasn't out of the ordinary. A lot of it was water weight, so most of it would sweat right off. It would be the last couple pounds that I'd have to work hard to cut. As the Games were quickly approaching, you could see all the fighters were locked in.

Many of us were fending for ourselves during training, much like we had to in Burnaby. Taylor Gordon and his team of coaches were not giving equal attention to all the fighters. They were putting all their time and effort into the "big-name" fighters that were on the team—names like Lennox Lewis, Egerton Marcus and Raymond Downey. It was bull, but I couldn't let it discourage me. When I won the gold medal, I'd make sure they didn't get any of the credit.

I didn't care who they were going to throw in front of me, but there were two opponents I would have loved to face. I was hoping to get the chance to take on Kelcie one more time. In reality, I could be 2-0 against Kelcie. Our previous fight outcomes wouldn't matter if I could beat him on this stage. I'd also have loved to get my hands on the Irishman, Paul Fitzgerald. That guy didn't deserve the decision over Steve, so I'd have loved to get some revenge.

During the weigh-ins, I actually ended up running into Fitzgerald. I could see his pasty skin from across the room. I still can't believe that the judges robbed Steve of a chance at a medal. I approached Fitzgerald when he got closer to where I was standing. I asked, "You're Paul Fitzgerald, aren't you?"

He replied, "So, are you here to avenge your brother's loss?"

Part of me wanted to rip into him and tell him what I thought about his style of fighting. I was able to hold my tongue and simply replied, "If we meet in the ring, that'll be the case." We never spoke again after that exchange.

The night before my fight, I could feel myself starting to get nervous. I still had no idea who I was fighting and that was freaking me out. My coaches weren't keeping me updated; my coaches weren't telling me anything. It just felt like it was going to be a rushed mess.

I walked to the bathroom and splashed some water in my face. I looked in the mirror and talked to myself. Why am I so scared? Uncertainty scares the hell out of me. I reminded myself of my goals, the goals I'd had since I started boxing twelve years ago. This was supposed to be my destiny. I wanted to be standing in the middle of the ring, with my hands held high, as the best fighter in the world. It started tomorrow. Tomorrow would be the day I fight at the 1988 Olymp—

Present Day

I abruptly close the photo album that's been taking me down this roller coaster of a journey. I look at the clock; it's three in the morning. I've had a few drinks, but I still feel stone-cold sober. I just relived my entire career leading up to the moment that changed it all. *Do I want to watch the fight?* I'm not sure anymore. Part of me does. Part of me is scared of how I'll react. *What if this sends me on another downward spiral?*

I walk away from the boxes and go to the bathroom. I turn the sink on to wash my hands. I want to refresh myself. I splash my face with the cold water several times. After the water drips off my face, I open my eyes and stare at my reflection. I'm still the same man from 1988 who was nervous about the uncertainty of the next day. Only difference is I'm thirty years older, and I'm still dealing with my demons.

Where did the champ go? It's crazy how a few moments in time can change the way you live out the rest of your existence. I feel like I've lost control of the wheel. I'm letting these moments control and dictate major aspects of my life.

No more.

I walk confidently into the rec room, grab the video from 1988. I decide to embrace pain as my partner.

CHAPTER XIII

The Fight

September 19, 1988

Leading up to the first Olympic fight of my career, there was a lot of anxiety building up inside of me. I'm not sure if it was because of the significance of the stage I was going to be performing on or if it was just the uncertainty of who my opponent would be in my first fight.

Much like my brother Steve, I would be the first Canadian boxer stepping into the ring to represent my country. While that is an honor for any warrior, it gives you less time to prepare properly. It was the same situation for both fighters competing in this particular fight, so it was all fair game.

It definitely would have been beneficial to have a little more time to feel out the environment and get an idea of how the whole Olympic set-up was going to work. It is what it is though. Some of the preparation I do before a fight is mental. I like to visualize the competitor across from me and how I can use my skills to pick him apart. It's incredibly difficult to do that when you have no idea who you are going to fight.

To a casual fan watching a match, they might just see two guys going toe-to-toe, throwing punches and trying to score points or knock each other out. While that is obviously the main objective, there are the smaller details like the fighter's stance and fighting style that play a huge role in my preparation.

I had no clue who I was going to be standing in the ring with, and it disrupted my usual pre-fight rituals. My attitude going into every fight was pure confidence, and I fed off of that self-belief. It's hard to feel confident when you're about to face your most important challenge, and you're in an unfamiliar set of circumstances. It was the Olympics! The best of the best compete here, and I was part of that. But it was unlike anything I'd ever experienced before. It's hard to not let doubt creep in.

Even though it was only the first fight, the stakes had never seemed higher. Every fight I had competed in for the past ten years had led me to this amazing opportunity. Winning an Olympic medal would show everyone what I already knew: that I deserved to be mentioned among the best, not just in Canada but the entire world. I actually had the chance to fulfill what I believe is my destiny. In a few moments, I would have the opportunity to see a ten-year dream come to fruition.

As a boxer, being at the Olympics is my Super Bowl, my Game Seven of the Stanley Cup finals. Once I stepped into the ring, I would forever have my name in the history books. No one handed me any of this; I had to earn this each and every step of the way. I knew all I had to do was grab it and take it, and no one would be able to deny me again.

Gordon and Napper finally informed me who my first opponent was going to be: a Mongolian fighter named Tserendorji Amarjargal. Mongolian fighters are tough as nails, and I have a lot of respect for how dangerous they can be in the ring. Coach Gordon very quickly went over some in-ring strategies with me as I was getting my hand wraps done.

Don't trade with the Mongolian, feel him out. Use your speed and footwork to open him up, and then land your punches. Footwork and speed will be important in this match.

Footwork and speed were my bread and butter. It was reiterated to me that the Mongolian was very aggressive and liked to come forward and pressure. That's where my footwork and counter-punching were going to come in to play. The coaches didn't want me to get into a slugfest with Amarjargal; they wanted me to use my talent and skill to out box him on the outside. That way I would control the fight.

Now that I knew who my opponent was going to be, I was able to finally visualize the bout. I could feel my gloves sinking into his body as I smoothly slipped past his aggressive rushes. I could visualize him standing in front of me, a fellow southpaw, throwing similar combinations at me, but not connecting them as cleanly as I do. I went through multiple scenarios, and it helped me get focused, even though I was forced to rush through my traditional preparation. It was time to go out there and fight.

I don't want to say it, but I was a bit unsettled. I did feel ready, but I definitely didn't like how unorganized and unprepared everyone was. In fact, it kind of pissed me off. Coach Taylor didn't even do a warm-up with me. No hand pads, nothing. But Taylor never did hand pads with any of the fighters, not even in the gym. I guess he was too good for that.

With my body glistening in a small layer of sweat, I made my way to the Olympic ring. The atmosphere in the building felt like nothing I'd ever experienced before. It had nothing to do with the crowds, although there were a lot of people watching. It is how I would imagine feeling if I were walking out of the tunnel for the Super Bowl. There were feelings of anxiety, feelings of adrenaline, and my anticipation was through the roof.

Although I didn't want to let the lights, the glitz and the glamor of the moment distract me from my task at hand, I couldn't help but take a moment and enjoy the feeling. It's a very human and humbling experience when you can look around and know that the moment in time is important.

It's the Olympics; what an achievement for anybody who gets the chance to compete on this stage. It's the best athletes each country has to offer, and we all deserve a fair shot to make our nations proud. All these thoughts are fine and dandy, but this didn't mean anything to me unless I came home with a medal. I forced myself to snap back to the proper mindset. *I hope you enjoyed those few seconds of reflection, Jamie, because it's time to get your head in the game and remember why you're here!* All of my mental energy was now refocused on my opponent as I approached the ring confidently.

The way they had the boxing area set up was extremely problematic. There were two rings in close proximity to one another, in order to present two matches simultaneously. At the time I didn't really put much thought into it; I had other things running through my mind.

My coach stepped on the bottom rope and pulled the middle one up for me to easily enter the Olympic ring. Everything was flying by like I was fast-forwarding through time. It was all a blur. I was so amped up at that point, I just wanted to start throwing punches immediately. I somewhat patiently waited for the announcer to go through the motions of introducing the fighters and, before I knew it, the bell had sounded.

The Mongolian approached the center of the ring from his blue corner, and I met him there. I found myself settling in early. Even though the stage was large and all eyes felt like they were watching me, eventually it began to feel like just a regular fight.

Despite the fact that neither fighter was fully engaging in their game plan, I still felt strong in round one. I would chalk up the hesitant first round to just wanting to feel each other out. However, I still knew that I needed to land my punches, score points and win every round I could.

We were both southpaws, so that changes the whole complexion of the fight right there. Southpaws often try to land the same punches and the same combinations, so it can be kind of awkward. Amarjargal did land a couple shots on me so I was able to feel the kind of zing he had on his punches. It was respectable, and I could see why my coaches didn't want me to risk getting into a slugging match with this fighter.

The bell went off, and we both went to our respective corners. Coach Gordon believed I won a close first round, but wanted me to get a little busier in the second. He liked the way I was picking my spots and boxing this guy.

Keep killing him with your footwork. You're gonna catch him with that hook, Jamie. Keep boxing this guy. Don't lose focus and don't let your guard down.

The commentator doing the broadcast of our match, Doug Saunders, agreed with my coach's thoughts on the first round, saying that if he was scoring the fight he would have given me a slight 20-19 edge in the first. Although winning rounds feels nice, I had no idea what the judges were thinking. Look at what happened to Steve in '84.

I didn't want to be on the wrong end of another bad decision. Especially when I knew I could take it out of the judge's hands and control my own destiny by punching this Mongolian's lights out. I knew if I could land my hook cleanly, he would taste the hard canvas. I knew I could hit hard. Doug Saunders even spoke highly of how hard I punched during the broadcast. He wasn't wrong when he said that my hands would be swollen and bruised from how much power I was laying behind my punches.

While the first round was mostly routine, the second round was everything but. The bell went off and, with a confident hop in my first couple steps, we once again met in the middle of the ring. Unlike the first round though, we engaged more aggressively. I threw the first jab of the round, and he quickly responded by extending his jab out. I was still very aware of my footwork and continued to circle the ring so as not to stagnate. I was trying to find my angles and slip a well-placed jab between his guard whenever I saw the opening.

I was timing his jab very nicely and countering with some head-snapping jabs of my own. This would be followed up with some combinations, and then I would disengage and continue using my footwork to find openings. After tasting his jab a few times, I would make sure he tasted mine immediately after.

Forty seconds into the round, the Mongolian attempted a weak hook to the body. I was able to easily slip the punch and land a stiff right jab to his chin. This staggered Amarjargal, his knee buckling as he took a step back. The ref stepped in between us and gave Amarjargal a standing eight count. A standing eight count occurs when the ref sees a fighter take a significant shot or when a certain amount of damage is inflicted. The eight count gives the fighter time to recover, but also gives the ref a chance to determine whether the fighter is okay to continue fighting.

I stood in my corner, staring into the Mongolian's eyes as the referee counted for what seemed like forever. I just wanted to get back in range so I could land some more blows to my dazed opponent. I knew the punch stunned him, but I didn't want to make a stupid mistake. Even though I would have loved nothing more than to go try and finish this guy right then, I had to be careful not to get caught with a shot going in too aggressively.

My confidence was through the roof after I stunned him. The next minute of the round was easily controlled by me. When we reengaged, I landed the next five punches unanswered. Jab, jab, jab. All clean shots right down the middle. Every shot he fired back at me was to no avail. I was deflecting every shot he threw my way with my gloves and my arms.

After throwing an overhand left hook, Amarjargal seemed to gain some momentum. He started throwing some combinations for the first time in the round. The left, then the right, then the left again. He was landing punches and pushing me backward a little bit. I found myself against the ropes taking multiple shots. My hands were up protecting my chin as best as I could, but I knew I couldn't sit there for long. I bullied my way back to the center of the ring and began fighting back against the pressure the Mongolian was putting on me.

The tempo of the fight was picking up. You could tell Amarjargal knew that he was in need of a big moment to make a comeback in the fight. Being down two rounds going into the third would require Amarjargal to pretty much have to knock me out. So it makes sense why he was amping up the quantity of punches he was throwing. The flurry of punches he landed in the last exchange woke up the sleeping confidence within Amarjargal.

The bell sounded for the end of round two. I began walking toward my corner, in my mind, up two rounds to zero on the Mongolian. This was until something bizarre happened: The referee yelled, "Keep fighting!" My corner yelled, "Keep fighting!" The Mongolian was still bouncing as if he had not heard the bell, completely engaged in the fight, while I had dropped my hands and dropped my guard.

I was extremely confused but didn't know how to properly react. I just listened to what they told me, put my hands back up and tried to refocus. The very next punch I threw was a jab, but the very next thing I remember was lying on the floor. Amarjargal slipped that jab and landed a one-two combination that sent me falling backward. I went from thinking the second round was over to, five seconds later, being flat on my back. I was only stunned though. What the heck just happened?

Well, unfortunately, since the two boxing rings were so close in proximity, you could hear the bell go off during the other fight and I mistook it as our bell. I had never been in a situation where there had been another fight going on right next to the ring I was competing in. It was definitely an issue the Olympic committee seemed to overlook.

I rolled over onto my side and shook my head to try to get rid of the stunned feeling. I could hear the ref counting, so I quickly got up to my feet and showed the ref I was ready to get back into the fight. My hands went right back up, and I entered back into the war zone.

I don't know why people do this, but when you've been knocked down, or even hurt in general, you always want to overcompensate to show that you're okay. It's kind of like when you come home drunk when you're a teenager and you try to hide it from your parents by doing your best to appear sober.

I knew that punch put me on the ground, and my head had a slight ring, but I was ready to go. I wasn't in any trouble. For the next few seconds though, as we engaged in combat mid-ring, I had an extra jump in my movements. I don't know if it was to show everyone watching that the punch didn't affect me, or if I just wanted to get right back into the fight by getting myself moving around again. Either way, it must've worked because I threw a nice long jab, which was followed by another quick, booming right hand that put Amarjargal right back on his backside six seconds after he had knocked me down.

He dropped fast and hard, like a ton of cement bricks. The Mongolian sat up. You could tell that I really clocked him good. If it was a cartoon, there would have been stars spinning around his head. When he got up, he was still showing signs of dizziness and unstableness. His first couple steps were wobbly and weak.

I was literally jumping up and down in my neutral corner. When I smell blood in the water, I've been known to pounce on my opponent and finish him. I couldn't wait to smack this guy with a few more combinations and put him right back where I just had him. I eagerly approached my opponent as I anticipated the continuation of the match. I was a little too eager, though; the ref made me back up again before he restarted the action.

There was about thirty seconds remaining in round two when the referee unleashed me back on my competitor. I could literally picture this fight ending any second now. Trouble was written all over him, and I wanted to finish it off with a beautiful exclamation mark. I walked him down like he was my prey and gave him a quick body shot followed by a thunderous right hook. The Mongolian fighter was retreating, but I didn't give him any room to breathe.

I smacked him with another right hook, then doubled up with another quick hook after that. As he continued to back up, I had him in my sights. I crushed him with yet another crippling right hook that bounced him right off the canvas again. He tried his best to stay on his feet, which is why he was able to get up so quickly. The way he landed against the ropes gave him some leverage to get up. If he had just lingered on the mat for a bit longer, I bet the ref would have felt compelled to end the match.

Regardless of how quickly he was able to get up, I knew how hurt this fighter was. He was on dream street, and I was keen on putting this guy away. I looked up at the clock quickly to see how much time I had left while the ref was still giving him a count. I had ten seconds left to unload one more explosive combination of hooks and, hopefully, avoid having to go to a third round.

Amarjargal looked like he was on skates, and I wonder if the round hadn't been so close to ending if the ref wouldn't have just stopped the fight right there. I unleashed one last flurry of punches on Amarjargal, hitting him flush again, and then the second round ended. I hit him a couple times after the bell had gone, because the crowd was cheering so loud that I couldn't even hear it. I stared him down and had a little cocky jump in my back step as I made my way to the corner. Other than the bell mishap that sent me to the canvas, I had a fantastic round. However, the fight should have already been over.

In a just world, the ref would have waved his hands in the air and ended the fight. In a fair world, one of the many judges sitting ringside would have jumped up onto the side of the ring and notified the referee that the fight was officially over.

In a perfect world, Hank Boone wouldn't have been sitting in prison; he would have been coaching me in my corner, screaming at the top of his lungs that the fight was over just like he did that very day from the prison he was incarcerated in. In a perfect world, they would have been able to hear Franny and Steve jumping up and down in their respective homes, screaming with joy in victory because they knew that the fight was over. My wife, who had never boxed a day in her life, saw something that the officials working at one of the most prestigious and well-respected sporting events in the world had blatantly missed.

I should have been in the center of the ring hearing my name being announced as the winner and the one moving on to the next stage of Olympic fights. Granted, a lot of things happened in round two. Among those things was me knocking Amarjargal down to the canvas twice, as well as forcing a standing eight count in the beginning stages of the round. That amounts to three knockdowns. Three is the magic number here.

Three eight counts in any same round means the fight is officially over according to amateur boxing's rules. In all the excitement, I didn't even realize I had administered three eight counts in the second round. I wasn't counting the knockdowns; I was focused on making sure I finished this guy when he was hurt. Even the commentator didn't realize, mistakenly calling my third knockdown the second knockdown of the round. With all the chaos that ensued during the second round, the first standing eight count given to Amarjargal was a forgettable moment. With that being said, many people didn't do their jobs that day. None of this was going through my head while I sat in the corner; I was too pumped up about what I had just accomplished that round. As I sat in my corner, I knew I won that last round. My corner congratulated me on my strong round but also fed me strategies to keep my mind focused on the fight we were still very much participating in. I had to relax and fight smart for this final round. I couldn't take my foot off the gas pedal, but I also didn't need to take any unnecessary risks. It's scary to leave it in the judges' hands though, as we've learned too many times before.

Every time I connected cleanly on this guy's chin, I hurt him badly. I was one solid hook or jab away from solidifying my first Olympic victory. My conditioning was on point, as I barely needed any time to catch my breath. By the time the third round bell was about to go off, I felt just as fresh as when the match had started, and I was ready to box this guy into submission for three more minutes or less.

I started the third round the same way I started the last two rounds, throwing the first punch and setting the pace. I thought if I could throw a few jabs, whether they hit him or not, it would throw him off his rhythm to start the round. Amarjargal was aware of where he stood on the score cards at this point, so it was important for me to be very conscientious and protect my chin with strong defense.

After backing up with a few quick jabs, Amarjargal was ready to plant himself right in the center of the ring and trade shots with me. I made sure I was light on my toes, constantly bouncing, so I could jump in and out of range easily. I was able to avoid the first few punches, but he wasn't really throwing anything out there that spelled any danger for me as of yet. When he missed a jab, I jumped in and landed a straight jab right through his guard. His head snapped back, and I began feeling the same confidence I felt near the end of the second round.

We continued to throw jabs at one another as we circled the smallest area right in the middle of the ring. Neither of us wanted to give the other one an inch. Sometimes an inch is all it takes to slide in there and steal a victory.

He was an aggressive fighter like my coaches warned me about and, while I was starting to feel confident in round three, Amarjargal was beginning to feel urgency and desperation. Knowing that he needed to make something happen, he began pushing forward, breaking up our game of ring-around-the-rosie and backing me up toward the ropes.

I was still getting my punches out there to keep him honest. Another jab of mine landed just under the fighter's chin. As I brought my hands back up, Amarjargal found his inch. The Mongolian surprised me with a popping right hand, and I fell backward, eventually staring at the ceiling as I lay on the mat.

It definitely stung, but it was nothing more than just a stinger. It was a good shot that knocked me down, but it didn't land flush on the chin. It landed more so around the bridge of my nose so, while it hurt me, it wasn't a knockout punch by any means. My hand was on the bottom rope and I used it to begin my ascent back up onto my feet. By the time I had gotten to a standing position, I felt like I had pretty much recovered and was clear minded. I thought, *If it's anything like the last time he knocked me down, his ass will be on the mat within the next few punches.*

It was strange because the ref touched my arm when I was almost on my feet. I remember wondering why I didn't hear him giving me an eight count. The ref ushered me to my corner, where I thought he was going to conduct his eight count. I'm still bouncing on my toes at this point because I'm ready to continue fighting. Coach Gordon stands up on the mat with his hands up in confusion. The ref says he is stopping the fight.

What do you mean, you are stopping the fight? That moment was crushing. To know I was not hurt or in any state of disarray, and for the fight to be taken away from me, was devastating. When I knocked down Amarjargal last round, he was literally stumbling around like he stayed at the bar until last call.

The fact that I didn't even get an eight count is a sick, disgusting joke.

The second my back hit the mat, the ref had already made a decision that I could not continue competing. That was complete negligence and extremely disappointing at this level of competition. The ref tried to explain to me his decision while he had me held up in my corner. I pushed the referee away from me and started moving around the ring in an effort to show him I was still very much aware and capable of continuing this fight. The ref watched me for a few seconds, before leaning over the top rope, and letting the judges know his decision.

I raised my arms angrily in the air and walked back toward my coaches. But not before I gestured at the ref and let him know what I thought about his decision to stop the fight. Amarjargal already had his headpiece off and was leaning up against his blue corner, raising his hand in victory as his coaches patted him on the back. The ref made his way to each side of the ring and told the judges he had stopped the match due to a blow to the head.

This was very confusing for me to understand, as I was immediately back on my feet and showed no clear signs of peril. I couldn't stop shaking my head in the corner. I couldn't even look at the ref. I'd look over my shoulder and tried to make eye contact with him, and he wouldn't look at me. He looked awkward as he went around telling the judges his decision, and, I believe, it's because he knew he screwed this one up.

I kept thinking to myself that this couldn't be the way that it ended. I held on to a dim hope that someone was going to rush to the ring and restart the fight. Even when the ref had us in the middle of the ring, announcing the winner officially, I held out hope for a break to go my way. I'm not the kind of guy who can ever catch a break. I'm not the glamorous American fighter, destined to go pro. I'm not the popular media darling that wins over fans at press conferences. I'm the small-town St. Catharines fighter, who sometimes feels like an afterthought. I had to fight for every ounce of respect I ever got. My break wasn't coming today. It began to really sink in as I left the ring. The match was over, the Olympics were over and my dream was over.

I had a lot of emotions running through my head after the fight. It was a rush of sadness, regret, anger and some other emotions mixed in there as well. Not only did I find myself with a loss, but it was a loss in the very first match. I didn't want to walk back to the locker room. I didn't want to believe that I was walking back to the locker room without a victory.

When I get beat in a match, I can accept that; but when you take it away from me, that's something no competitor takes lightly. As I walked past the fans, officials and other athletes, I felt isolated with this disgusting feeling trapped in my stomach. My coaches trailed behind me as we approached the tunnel. I knew I was representing my country and that I had to say the right things and do the right things, but I was reaching a boiling point. With my gloves still on, I turned in the tunnel and violently punched the wall before my coaches ushered me further into the darkness toward our locker room. Something was not right here. I was about to find out that this fight was a whole lot more controversial than I even realized at that point.

CHAPTER XIV

Buried Alive

September 19, 1988

Franny Pagendam

Jamie's fight was airing at 6:30 a.m. our time and only on the French station. My cousin Anthony and my friend Laura slept over so they could wake up and watch the fight with me in the morning. We were watching and watching, and I caught the third eight count in the second round. I looked at Anthony and said, "The fight should be over." Anthony questioned whether there was a different set of rules for the Olympics. The fight had carried on, so I thought maybe the rules could be different then.

When the fight was stopped in the third round, we were pissed because we were pretty sure the fight should have already ended. It was hard to know what was going on because the commentary was in French. It wasn't until later that we were able to watch the fight in English on the CBC. In the second round of the replayed version, the commentator yells, "The fight should be over! The fight should be over!" Of course, they already knew all that had happened. The original English broadcast of the fight totally missed the third knockdown.

As all this was going on, no one was doing anything for Jamie in Korea because he had no family or friends with him. I tried to do something on my end. I contacted our lawyer at the time, Dennis Gross, who sent over a wire to Korea saying that if they didn't review the tapes of the fight that we were going to proceed with legal action against the organizers of the Olympic committee.

I don't know what ever happened with that wire, but the whole situation was wild. Reporters were hounding me nonstop. I remember one reporter asking me what I thought about the decision, and the next day the newspaper headline said, "I THINK THE DECISION STINKS" in big bold letters.

I had to take a couple days off work. It was mostly so I could call Jamie, make sure he was okay and get him home safely; but it was also because the attention we were getting was too much. It was absolutely draining. When I finally did end up going back to work, I had to hide in the back room because reporters were waiting in the store to ask me questions. It was scary. My phone at home didn't stop ringing, the phone at work didn't stop ringing; it was a total nightmare.

Jamie Pagendam

I was extremely confused. From the moment the ref stopped the bout, it felt like I was in a mirror maze. I couldn't escape the feeling, and I hated dwelling on it. The worst part was that no one was saying anything to me. No one was able to clear anything up for me. My initial thoughts were that the ref must have thought I was seriously hurt because he didn't even give me an eight count. To not even get an eight count, with a chance to recover, was unfair and unjust.

The walk back to the locker room felt like a century. The confusion I felt wavered between anger and disappointment. The first thing I said to my coaches when we finally reached the room was "You guys need to definitely protest the decision, because this is wrong. There's no way they should've stopped the fight."

The coaches protested the decision. Later, Taylor Gordon explained in an interview that the contest was unfair and that we, as a team, believed the fight was stopped for the wrong fighter. This all took place fairly quickly after the match; therefore, at this point, none of us were even aware that there had been three eight counts in the second round. The fight should never have gone to a third round. That's what we should have been protesting.

I was thrown in front of the media right away (still having no knowledge of the three eight counts). None of the reporters asked me about it, meaning they didn't recognize what had transpired either. I just humbly answered their questions and threw blame toward the ref stopping the fight early with no explanation.

It wasn't until later on in the afternoon, when I was walking around the arena, that I would find out some facts about the fight that were flying right over our heads. A newspaper reporter came up to me and pulled me aside. He asked, "Why didn't they stop the fight after the third eight count?" I shook my head, confused, and replied, "What are you talking about? This is news to me."

I don't know who this reporter was, but he had picked up on the three eight counts. He went over the events of the second round and pointed out three times the ref gave the Mongolian fighter an eight count. I didn't know what to think. How did so many people miss this? The reporter said he talked to Taylor Gordon earlier and that he had refused to watch the tapes.

I knew right away that I now had a very viable protest to bring to the table. Of course, Taylor Gordon was nowhere to be found during all of this. He went off somewhere. I wasn't even able to be in contact with Gordon during this. Eventually, he was shown the footage, and he had no choice but to see the mistake he had made in missing the three eight counts. So they filed a protest under the assumption that the fight should have been terminated in the second round. I felt like there was a huge glimmer of hope because we had proof that the rules of boxing weren't followed correctly.

Once all this new information was beginning to come to light, Taylor Gordon finally reemerged. He asked to speak privately with me for a minute so we went behind closed doors. He seemed a little nervous, but everyone was on edge that day. He began to overwhelmingly stress not to say anything bad about him to anybody, especially in front of the media. He didn't say anything about protecting Ray Napper. He just straight up asked me to not say anything bad about him on TV or to the media, because he could get in trouble. I didn't understand the magnitude of the situation and had no idea what the outcome of this protest was going to be, so I assured him I wouldn't say anything negative to the media.

The awful thing about this whole situation was that he was more concerned about covering his own butt than he was about getting me in a position to continue my Olympic journey for Canada. Like I said before, the man never apologized, ever, about what had transpired. He was supposed to be my coach and have my back, and he missed such a crucial part of the match. That was his job. Nobody wanted to be held accountable, so the blame kept getting shifted down to the next person.

I held back on putting any blame on my coaches the best that I could. Even when I was interviewed by the big television networks like NBC and CBC, I didn't throw my coaches under the bus. They tried their hardest to get a quote from me, but I bit my tongue really hard.

It had been a wild two days. While I was in the oven sweating, someone else I knew had gotten burned. A couple hours after I had my first fight, I heard a loud pop from the crowd while I was standing near the media room. I turned the corner and saw Kelcie Banks knocked out cold in the center of the ring by the hands of Regilio Tuur of the Netherlands.

Kelcie and I were competitors, but we had a lot of respect for one another. So when he was being helped out of the ring and toward the locker room area with his coaches and managers, I walked over to him and put my arms around him. I said, "It's going to be okay." I held him for only a second, but you could feel the emotion pulsating from his body. I just knew how he felt. His world was crashing down on him, and the emotions can drown you.

The next day, in the Olympic Village, we got something to eat and had a conversation about life, boxing and life after boxing. At the time, my protest was still unresolved. Kelcie told me, a month or two before the Olympics, he was offered a huge deal to turn professional. The U.S. Olympic Boxing Association coerced him to stay. They dangled the carrot in front of him by telling him a gold medal would make that pro deal so much more lucrative. My goal was to turn professional after the Olympics too, but only if I won a medal. You're more marketable that way.

He was the best amateur in the world coming into the Olympics, but he knew losing like that was going to affect his professional deal. Needless to say, he was a great fighter. We had great comradery and built a friendship after we both lost. In my opinion, we were two of the top four or five boxing prospects at the Olympics that year. We were medal favorites, but sometimes it just doesn't work out the way you want it to.

I didn't know my legal rights and the impact this would ultimately have on my life down the road. I was just trying to be the good guy and protect those around me. It was exhausting having to go through this entire endeavor. Through it all, I had no help whatsoever from the Canadian contingent. They put in a protest on my behalf, which was a no-brainer. Other than that, I was naked and vulnerable for the whole world to pick apart.

After we submitted the protest, certain events were set in motion. The people in charge of reviewing protests deemed that the ref should have ended the fight during the second round and that I should have been named the winner. As long as I passed my physical, everything was looking good in terms of my continuation at the Olympics.

My medical exam consisted of a few different tests, including a CAT scan of my brain. Every test they threw my way, I passed it no problem. Everything checked out, and I was officially cleared for competition. It was a day and a half after my fight that I stood in front of the protest committee and was notified that they had reversed the decision. They awarded me the victory and were going to allow me to continue on at the Games.

After getting the green light to fight again, it had felt like a weight had been lifted off my shoulders. I had overcome the adversity being forced upon me, and it felt like nothing was going to stop me now. It had been an eventful two days, but things were beginning to calm down as events were set straight. The media was still very interested in my story, but after I gave my initial reaction to the reversal, they started to slowly shift toward other news.

It was nice to be able to sleep comfortably again. The nights prior went by so slowly. But now the second my head touched the pillow, I was out like a light. I didn't wake up once during that evening's sleep and only had positive dreams throughout. I felt like getting the decision reversed was going to be the hardest opponent I faced at the Games. I wasn't wrong either.

I proudly put on my Canadian-themed track pants, accompanied by a white undershirt and proceeded to jog down to the training facility for my morning workout. There were smiles all around as I ran through the Village. It was a cloudy day, but you could still see the sun cracking through the holes in the clouds. I felt light on my feet and clear minded.

A familiar face awaited me as I strolled up to the front doors of the gym. It was the same newspaper reporter who had first notified me of the fact that there were three eight counts in the second round. Very much like the first time I encountered him, he was the only one around.

He wanted to ask me a couple questions if I didn't mind giving him a second of my time. I didn't know what he could possibly ask that hadn't been published in the news already.

He asked me what I thought about the Amateur International Boxing Association (AIBA) sticking with their decision to overturn the victory to me but not allowing me to further participate in the tournament. I said, "What are you talking about? The protest committee overturned the decision and is allowing me to fight. I passed my medical exams, I'm good."

The reporter told me that they had changed their minds. The president of AIBA, Anwar Chowdhry, disallowed me to continue due to what the referee had called head blows.

The ironic thing about it was that the referee who worked my match, Joseph Lougbo, was suspended from the Olympic Games because of the awful mistake he made. They suspended him indefinitely for his incompetence, yet they stood by his initial ruling of the fight ending due to head blows. They did offer him a role as a judge for the remainder of the Games, but Lougbo refused because he didn't have his glasses, and he couldn't see without his glasses. How great is that?

According to AIBA rules, fighters whose bouts are stopped due to head blows may not compete for 60 days. I just don't understand how they can kick a ref out of the Olympics for being incompetent but still stand by his decision. I was clearly fine after I got knocked down. I was right back on my feet and ready to go, not to mention I passed all my medical exams. I was fuming.

When I found out about this new development, it took another strip off of me. It's like having a bandage ripped off, and then someone picking at the scab that's formed. It just kept digging deeper, and it felt like the wound was never going to stop cutting into me. I was just totally beside myself. The worst part was having no family or friends in Korea. I was completely heartbroken.

After I stood outside the gym for a while, I gathered my bearings and slammed through the doors. Why in the world was I finding out about this from a news reporter? Where were my coaches? Where was the accountability?

When I walked into the gym, it was like everyone stopped. It didn't stop dead, but it was like everyone slowed down in anticipation of my arrival. I made a beeline for Ray Napper because, of course, Taylor Gordon wasn't there. I knew Ray knew, because the second he saw me come in, he dropped everything he was doing with his fighter and acknowledged me.

I said, "Ray, what's going on?"

He kinda hemmed and hawed and replied, "Yeah, Jamie, I didn't know how to tell you."

That pissed me off. "What do you mean, you didn't know how to tell me? This is my life, this is my Olympic dream, and you don't know how to tell me?"

Ray stood there as I blew off some steam. He didn't know how to respond so I turned and just walked away. I was done with all of this.

I gathered my belongings, shoved them in my gym bag and made my way to where I knew the Canadian contingent was meeting. All the important individuals who represented the Canadian athletes made up this group, and I wanted to hear it from the horse's mouth, so I approached them. I said, "What's going on with this? One day I can fight, now they're telling me I can't. What's going on here?"

They said I wasn't allowed to continue because the ref wrote down that he stopped the fight due to head blows. I argued that they awarded me the win. They acknowledged that the win got overturned, but they weren't really showing any interest in putting up a fight against the ruling.

I said, "Well, that's just great. What am I supposed to do now?"

They said if I wanted to go home they could get me an airline ticket for the next day. I quickly replied, "Get me outta here." I had to leave; I couldn't be there anymore. How could I stay and support this, knowing what they'd done to me and my life?

Believe me, everyone was happy to see me go. My whole situation was a giant distraction for everyone on the Canadian boxing team. They didn't want me in the public eye anymore.

Everything was about me. All the questions were about me. I know Taylor Gordon and the other Canadian officials were happy to see me go. They knew eventually someone would get to me and make me crack, and I would spill my guts to the world.

Taylor Gordon avoided me like the plague during those three days. I strictly communicated with the Canadian Olympic Association's figure heads and Ken Napper, the team manager. I had to maneuver my way through all of this primarily on my own, and I was only twenty-two years old.

Arriving Home, September 1988

I looked out the window as the plane finally landed on the tarmac. It felt like a relief to be back at home, but in the back of my mind, I was wondering what everyone's reactions were going to be. Really, the only thing that mattered at this point was seeing my beautiful wife. I knew life was going to feel weird for a little while but, as long as I had Fran by my side, I was going to make it through.

The media in Canada was far crazier than it was back in Korea. Every news outlet was covering my story. My face was on every newspaper, and I was on the news every day during the sports segment. This was the most attention I had ever been given in my entire life. We had to unplug the phone for a couple days because it just wouldn't stop ringing.

It slowed down a little after the Ben Johnson saga took over the mainstream media. I was still answering a slew of questions from people I was bumping into around the city. Any time I ran into an acquaintance or a co-worker, they wanted to talk about what had happened. Sometimes I didn't mind the attention, but sometimes I wasn't in the mood.

I didn't watch a whole lot of Olympic boxing after I returned home. If it was on TV, I would throw it on, but I wasn't particularly into it for obvious reasons. I just happened to be flipping through the channels when I stumbled upon an American, Todd Foster, who was about to take on Korean fighter Jin-Chul Chun. Foster was landing some clean, flush shots on Chun in the early stages of the fight. The match started out exciting, so I stopped channel surfing and continued to watch. Foster was easily winning the fight going into the third round.

As the third round was closing in on thirty seconds, the bell in the other ring sounded, exactly like it did in my fight. The fighters were engaged in tight combat as the bell sounded. Chun put his hands down and started walking to his corner. Foster was aware that the bell was from the other ring and smacked the Korean with a booming left hook. Chun didn't go down immediately but, eventually, after taking a couple steps, he dropped face-first to the mat. The ref began counting. The Korean kept looking up for some reason, then began rolling on the ground as if he had been shot. The referee counted a full ten, and the fight was called a knockout victory for Foster.

In boxing, whenever you get counted out, it's a knockout. That's a 90-day medical suspension. The referee counted the full ten seconds, and the Korean was still lying on the mat, not even attempting to return to his feet. Several people's account of the fight say that the Korean coach actually told Chun to drop to the mat in the hopes that something screwy might come of it. He flopped. The ref, Sandor Pajar, was suspended for the rest of the Olympics after he yelled "stop" when the other bell's ring sounded, so even the referee was confused by the sound of the other bell.

There's a lot to unpack here. Let me start by saying, the events that took place after this match pissed me off. This really paints a vivid picture of how corrupt and unjust sports can be. The Korean contingent and AIBA discussed the fight's events immediately afterwards, and it was decided that Foster and Chun would fight again two and a half hours later. I don't know what transpired behind closed doors for those two hours, but any outcome that resulted in anything different than what happened to me is a crime.

This is the same group of people who took days to review my tapes, then went back and forth on what they wanted to do with my situation. I passed extensive medical examination, which took them a full day to clear me through. AIBA then said I couldn't compete because the ref ended my fight due to head blows. The

Korean was on the mat for an entire ten count; the fight ended by knockout, yet, he got to fight again two and a half hours later.

The Canadians didn't even put up a fight about this. These two situations are almost identical. The main difference is that it would've made a heck of a lot more sense for me to continue than for the Korean to get a rematch that same afternoon. For one, I actually won my match. We both technically had our matches end due to head blows, except I got up quickly with no count from the ref, and he laid flat on the mat for an entire ten seconds. It's also worth noting that I also got knocked down during a mishap with the bell. I didn't take a dive, but maybe I should have. My circumstances clearly, by far, constituted a more favorable outcome than that of the Korean fighter's. The fact that Chun's chances of fighting again at the Olympics should have been bleaker than mine and he got to fight two hours later is a slap in my face. The Games were held in Chun's country (the prejudice was there). Foster knocked his undeserving opponent out again, this time in the first round.

Needless to say, I was livid about the whole situation. This was one hundred percent political. I honestly could have sued everyone involved in this sham of an Olympics for the way they handled my fight, especially now, when paralleled with the Todd Foster fight. All the judges, the referee, my coaches, the Olympic committee—I could've taken them all down. But I didn't. I was young, I was stressed, and I just wanted it to all go away so I could move on with my life.

After I saw how the Foster/Chun fight was handled, I didn't want anything to do with the sport of boxing. That was the straw that broke the camel's back. Not right away, but these events were leading me to a downward spiral. Everything that had happened at the Olympics, the tough breaks, the stuff with Hank—it all piled on as I carried around years of baggage. Pain was my partner, but I never intended for him to become my best friend. I was slowly heading toward a very dark path.

What happened to me at the 1988 Olympics is the biggest controversy in Olympic sports history. A lot of athletes get caught using steroids or were caught cheating the system, but no athlete has ever been so horribly wronged by the actual Olympic Association. What happened to me at the '88 Olympics is the biggest controversy in Olympic sports history. Period.

CHAPTER XV

From Seoul to Salvation

My Lost Brother, 1988–1992

Steve Pagendam

Jamie was still very prominent in the public eye after his return from Seoul. Guys would invite him out for beers. He had a lot of people hanging on and riding his coattails. Although Jamie felt down about the outcome of his Olympic experience, the attention he was getting was softening the blow for the time being.

Upon returning from Korea, a lot of good things happened for Jamie. For one, he was recognized as the male athlete of the year in St. Catharines. With that, he got to go to a fancy banquet where they presented him with that honor, and he and his family enjoyed a lovely meal. Even though they all knew what had taken place at the Olympics, he was still getting recognized for being great in the sport. He was a big part of a parade they throw in St. Catharines every fall. The city did their best to make sure he felt appreciated for his accomplishment.

You could tell it ate away at him. He was getting recognition, but it wasn't the recognition he wanted. He only desired what he felt he deserved. He wanted a fair opportunity at a gold medal. He had all the abilities in the world to get there. All the recognition was only reminding him that he did a good job, but he still got ripped off. As time went on, it only became more apparent to Jamie that his dream had slipped away, and there was no going back to that dream ever again. Chasing after gold medals and sporting accolades can't last forever.

Sure, the alcohol and the parties cushion the blow, but once that was all stripped away from him he was left alone with his thoughts. That's when he started spiraling downward. I was in a different place than Jamie in almost every way. I had kids, I was going to church, I was older; he was still growing into his manhood. He still had some decisions ahead to be made. I tried to get my brother out to church, but he wanted nothing to do with God. I had seen the positive changes that occurred in my life after accepting Christ as my savior, and I wanted the same for my brother.

I could see his life becoming destructive. I could feel his heart wasn't at peace. Even though I found myself distanced from Jamie, I was always thinking about him and hoping he was okay. As much as I loved my brother and cared for him, his whole attitude put us at odds with one another. During this time in our lives, I didn't see Jamie nearly as much as I once did.

The only way I could really have a relationship with my brother was if I went and watched him play hockey with his Merritton buddies. I would sit in the stands and watch, and after the games he would give me a quick wave from the bench. Then he was off to the bar with his teammates. I knew how often he was at the bars, because guys I worked with at GM would often tell me they saw my brother at the bar last night. I also was getting updates from Franny occasionally.

There were nights where Jamie didn't even tell Fran he was going to the bar after work, and she would call me frantically worried. I would be out looking for him, checking all the bars he usually went to until I found him. I'd walk in, and Jamie would sarcastically say, "Here comes my big brother Steve to rescue me." He'd tell me to turn around, tell me he was fine and that he wasn't leaving yet. This was sometimes a weekly endeavor.

I wanted more for Jamie's life. I wanted him to have a relationship with God. Like I said, there is more to life than chasing after gold medals. There's a quote in the Bible that says, "For what shall it profit a man, if he shall gain the whole world, and lose his own soul?" In Jamie's way of thinking, the Christians were wimps. I was a wimp to him because of what I believed. He had completely shut out anything to do with Christianity and was dead-set on living life the way he wanted to.

I was spending a lot of time praying for Jamie. When I was working at General Motors, during our lunch hour, a group of us would get together in a room and pray for our family members. We would spend a lot of time praying for Jamie. Some of the guys knew my brother, and they would pray for him independently too. I would lay awake at night sometimes, just hoping and praying that something would speak to Jamie's heart and show him the way.

My Husband's Mind, 1988–Present

Franny Pagendam

Immediately after the Olympics, even though he was really disappointed with the outcome, he wasn't feeling too down in the dumps because everyone was rallying around him. Everyone was boosting him up because he was the star. He got letters from all over Canada sending well wishes and sharing displeasure for how Jamie got shafted. The story was still running in all the papers, discussing the controversy and praising how Jamie handled it all. He was getting a lot of attention from many different circles, and it was keeping his mind occupied.

Jamie got back into sports by joining a hockey team with some of his old Merritton friends. They would play their hockey game, and then either go out to the bar or head over to someone's house to play cards until seven in the morning. I'd be stuck there because I'd have to drive him home. That's when he started getting into drinking a little bit.

He rarely had any booze during his boxing days. Once he didn't have to worry about training or making weight, having a few drinks wasn't an issue any longer. The drinking really started immediately after the Olympics. He was getting all the attention from people wanting to hear the story of what happened, and they would buy him drinks because he was kind of like a celebrity in the city. This led to Jamie's darkest years, but once he started cleaning up his act, something else was lingering around that was destructive in a different way.

Over a two-year period, I started noticing behavioral changes. They were all minor changes but, as his wife, I could see them all adding up. Many outsiders looking in might see certain things that he was doing or saying and then chalk it up to bitterness or entitlement. In reality, a lot of his behavior was directly linked to the way he was starting to perceive things. It was always about "someone said this" or "someone did that on purpose."

He started having issues with people in the workplace. It wasn't really bad at Fraser Paper Mill. The people there didn't bother him very much. When he got hired at National Steel Car, that's when the paranoia truly started. That company hired a lot of "tough customers" from around the province, and they were mean-looking, big dudes. He would come home and make comments about some of these guys walking behind him in the parking lot and feeling like they were going to do something to him.

National Steel Car was when I first started noticing these strange instances; however, when he got hired at Hayes Dana, it started getting even worse. Every conversation that happened around him or behind closed doors, he believed they were talking about him. Jamie also felt that his co-workers were conspiring to play tricks on him, and it was almost constant. Then it would stop for a couple weeks, and you wouldn't hear a single complaint from Jamie pertaining to his work relationships. Then, all of a sudden, it would all start up again, and it would be even more extreme than the last time.

Hayes Dana was a complete nightmare for him. He felt like he was a target, and I was very worried for him. I was worried, not because I thought he was a target, but because I didn't know how I was going to help him see that these people weren't after him. He was overthinking his interactions far too much.

It got a little easier for us when he started working for Coach Canada, because he was mostly dealing with tourists all day. These people didn't know Jamie, and he was aware of that, so he felt comfortable most days. He'd still have his moments with people outside of his employment, but it wasn't as intense as the previous jobs he had.

While he was still working at Coach Canada, he took a leave of absence to work in the Thorold tunnel, which was very similar to National Steel Car (lots of convicts and rough, edgy people). One of his really good friends and our close neighbor for many years, Carmen, got him the job. They worked closely together. As time went on at this job, you could see the way he thought about Carmen was changing. He thought Carmen was conspiring with some of the other workers against him. I had to be like, "Jamie, this guy's like your brother. He's not going to do anything to hurt you." I felt deep down Jamie knew that, but he couldn't help the thoughts that were bouncing around in his brain.

Many of the comments he didn't like had to do with boxing. He felt like as soon as some of the guys knew he was an Olympic boxer, they wanted a piece of him. They would make comments like, "Hey Jamie, wanna go?", and he would see it as a threat, when really it wasn't at all. It was just guys joking around with him on the site. I remember pulling my hair out on a daily basis trying to explain to him that the things he was thinking were not the way they were happening.

When he eventually couldn't handle being down in the tunnel any longer, he went back to driving a bus. He found out about an opening at St. Catharines transit as a bus driver. When he first started at transit, he was fine. A couple months went by, and you could start seeing his thought process changing again. He began consistently showing the same patterns of paranoia and distrust that he had at the other jobs.

He started wondering how people perceived him and what their motives were. When someone said something to him, even just a meaningless piece of conversation, you could see him start to try and decipher what they meant by it. Even to this day, you can see it. Text messages are the worst, and those are from people he knows and has some type of relationship with.

There were times when he'd get suspicious of some of my family or friends. He'd be thinking if he didn't get invited to go have a few beers on the porch or if we didn't get invited to an outing, it was because they didn't want him around so they could talk behind his back. It got to the point that when he was in their company, he'd have a shield up and they could sense it. Then Jamie would wonder why they were distancing themselves. I'd tell him, "It's because you're making them feel unwelcome and uncomfortable."

He just doesn't quite get why people say certain things sometimes. Like when he's driving the bus and there's only a few people riding. The passengers make ignorant or crude remarks to one another, and say very obnoxious things to each another. Jamie will overhear their conversation and wonder, "Why did they make that comment? Are they talking about me?" And I'll say, "No, that's just how people talk sometimes." Jamie doesn't get why people speak like that to each other. He has to remember, those people getting on the bus at the terminal, or anywhere out in public, might also be dealing with mental health issues too. We don't know what people are dealing with in their lives sometimes.

Something as simple as the way people wave to him or the way people smile at him can set him off. The way he was reacting to certain things was ultimately hurting his relationships with co-workers and friends. It was getting out of hand.

Seeing all these things taking place in Jamie's life was very concerning to me. I knew there was something wrong with him, and I needed to help him. I sent him to our family doctor after his first real mental breakdown, which happened during his time at the tunnel. He was able to set up an MRI for Jamie. The results showed that he had lesions on the front of his brain. Things started making a little more sense, but we needed to find a solution.

I set him up an appointment to meet with a psychiatrist, because he needed to learn how to deal with it properly on a daily basis. The brain injuries he sustained during his boxing career were affecting his thought process. They figured he had paranoid thought disorder. It was really bad. If Steve and myself weren't around him to be a buffer and to make him realize that what he was thinking was not real, who knows what he would've done. Honestly, he probably would have ended up being committed to a psychiatric facility. There were times he would spiral so bad that he couldn't even function. If he had kept getting worse, there would have been no chance he could have functioned in society.

His medication is important to keeping him stable. If he wasn't on his meds, he'd spiral. If they even lower his dosage, he starts to fall back into a spiral. For example, I could see it starting automatically when they had to change the brand of medication he was on, as recent as this past year. During the transition, you could see how his thought process gradually started changing, and the paranoia and distrust kicked in. It's that severe. But being properly medicated helps him function on a daily basis.

I think what happened to him at the Olympics definitely contributed to aspects of how he began thinking. The brain damage is the biggest factor, but you can't eliminate the clear ties to the Olympic controversy and his patterns of distrust among people. You have to factor in how the whole Hank situation went down as well. It's things like this that can easily trigger thoughts of doubt, distrust and paranoia. So yeah, I do believe it was a mix of the brain injuries and the disappointments that caused him to think the way he does.

It's hard to know how everything would have turned out if things had happened differently in his boxing career. He may have still started drinking with his hockey buddies, but maybe it wouldn't have become so bad. Maybe he would have still had mental health issues, but maybe they wouldn't have been so extreme and crippling. All I know is that what happened to him at the Olympics kind of made him feel like he could never be fully satisfied with the way his life turned out. That's what fed thoughts like, "If I had won the gold medal, I wouldn't have to work in a factory," "I wouldn't have issues with money," "things would have been easier," "things would have been different." Maybe they would have been.

Maybe if Jamie won the gold medal, things would have lined up the way he thinks they would have. But who's to say it would have been better? A lot of times people become famous, and they spiral just as bad, if not worse. Who's to say how life would have actually turned out? I always tell him, though, just be happy with what you have. We are blessed with what we have. Jamie loves his family so much. He shows us every day. We do everything we can to support him and help him, because we love him so much too.

From Seoul to Salvation, 1988–1992

Jamie Pagendam

I went back to work after letting the disappointments of the past three weeks soak in a little. A group of my co-workers surrounded me as I was punching in and they gave me a nice, long clap as a show of respect for what I had accomplished. Everybody wanted a piece of the Olympian. I got asked out for drinks on a daily basis, and it was hard to pass up a free meal and some cold ones to wash it down. I would call home and I would let Fran know I was going to grab a drink with some of the work boys.

After that was going on for a while, Franny made it known that she was getting tired of me going out after work every night. I would say, "Well, it'll only be for an hour or two." Eventually she would just be fine with it, and I would carry on with my evening.

Four or five hours would pass, and time would begin leaking into the middle of the night. I'd be pretty drunk, but I'd still get into my car and drive myself home after midnight. Franny would get mad at me for staying out so late, and we'd get into arguments over it. I didn't see anything wrong with going out with some co-workers after a long shift.

Even months after the Olympics, I was still finding comfort in going out for drinks with people who were boosting my ego. They'd buy me a drink and put their arm around me and say, "Oh man, Jamie, you got robbed man. You're still the champ, though, man. We're all proud of you." They wanted me to come down to the level they lived on, and I did.

I had only been married a year, so the lifestyle I was starting to live was totally conflicting with the life I had promised to Fran. But I had no idea how much damage I was really doing. I figured everyone understood what I was going through, so I'd have a bit of a grace period with my family and close friends. Being around people who were putting me on a pedestal, mixed with some drinks, was drowning my disappointments. I didn't want it to stop.

Eventually, the attention started to dissipate. People weren't asking me to grab a beer with them because I was an Olympic athlete; they were asking me to come out for drinks because I was their drinking buddy. They didn't even need to ask me anymore; I knew my way to the bar.

My job at the paper mill was taking a back seat to my addiction. I'd either go to work completely hungover, still intoxicated or I'd just call in sick. My dad still worked at Fraser, but he never sat me down and talked to me about what I was doing. I guess he just wanted to stay out of it, seeing as though I was an adult now. I wasn't making mature, adult decisions but, by definition, I was an adult.

The parades and celebration of the Olympian Jamie Pagendam soon became the pity-party for the drunken, punched-out boxer who's got nowhere to go. I'm pretty sure my dad had spoken to the manager of the mill because it wasn't long before I got called up to his office for a word. I was missing a lot of work, so I knew what the tone of this meeting was going to be like. The manager didn't mince words. He closed his door and immediately began screaming and shouting at me.

My eyes watered up with tears, because this man was not holding back. He said to me, "I don't know who you think you are, but in here you're a paper maker. I don't care if you've been to the Olympics or not. That means nothing to me. You have to show up for work, show up on time and be sober." The tears began rolling down my face. I wasn't used to being spoken to so sternly and aggressively. He continued, "The next time I call you up to this office, it will be for a dismissal."

My boss laid it on heavy and made it known that I wasn't special anymore. I was just another worker. So I cleaned up my act at work. I made an effort to show up on time, put in a full day's work, and I made sure I was sober on the job. I did just enough to appease my managers. I didn't really change anything I was doing outside of the mill, though. I continued to drink with co-workers and hockey buddies on a regular basis.

The drinking kept going even after I joined athletics again. The Merritton boys had a beer league team, and they asked me if I wanted to play. I thought it'd be a good way to keep myself in, at least, decent shape. I soon found out that it was just going to be another avenue to feed my addiction. We would drink in the locker room before and after the games. We would go out to Mister C's for food and more beer afterward. Our wives would come watch our games, and we'd make them wait out in the bleachers while we sat in the locker room for four hours, pounding back beers. I was just a young guy who thought he was having harmless fun.

I was a twenty-two-year-old young man, hanging around the bars like it was my home. I had men and women constantly reinforcing the fact that I had gotten shafted, but that I was still an icon in their eyes. The only time I would hear this medicating praise was when I went to the bars. I got sucked into this lifestyle, and it was what defined me now. Every time I walked in, I got an ovation from the regulars. I was drunk off the attention, which led to me getting drunk off the booze at the counter. People were excited to see me walk in, and they made it known.

It wasn't long before I switched from beer to hard liquor: whiskey, vodka, rum. I would drink anything to get the feeling I craved faster. I would down glasses of whiskey quickly because I was already looking forward to my next one. Once I started building relationships with the guys around the bar, they introduced me to the world of drugs. I was smoking pot and hash outside the bar to get high and drinking whiskey and rum inside to get wasted. My stomach would feel so sick that I would go into the bathroom and throw up just so I could continue drinking more. I was in a very dark world, but I wasn't missing the light in the slightest.

I would come home to Franny, who would be crying in the living room, and I'd get upset with her. "What are you crying for?" And she'd ask me, "Where have you been? Why didn't you come home last night? Why are you home so late? Who were you with?"

I was constantly lying to my wife. I didn't want to tell her where I was. Nobody could have understood why I was doing what I was doing. I don't even think I knew the real reason to why I was doing all of this.

Many times I would wake up in my bed not knowing when I had gotten home or how I had got there. I was an absolute mess of a man. It was making my wife's life a living hell. But she was as strong as a rock. Even though I know she was hurting on the inside, she never let it bring her down to my level. She would clean up my puke in the morning, she would help me stumble to bed when I'd burst through the door at three a.m., she would wake me up in the morning with breakfast. Even with all the crap I was putting her through, she stood by me. But she would beg me to stop every day. I just couldn't. I was in a black hole and the pain was just too much—even though, at the time, I didn't realize I was living in that kind of pain. It was my belief that this was the lifestyle I wanted to live.

Living this lifestyle made me forget everything. When you put six or seven drinks down the hatch, you start to not really care about anything. Everything is carefree, and I liked that feeling better than the pain. I looked forward to getting myself back into this mindset every night. It was an addicting way to live life. A lot of people didn't know this side of me. Many of my friends and family didn't know that I was out every night getting obliterated because I hid it. But the people in the dungeons and basements of the dark places knew me as a different person. I was a lost soul.

No one was there to guide me when I got back from the Olympics. My parents were dealing with their own stuff. I think my dad figured I'd grow out of it anyways. I don't know if he even knew the extent of what I was doing. I had distanced myself from Steve because I didn't want him to try and talk me out of the way I was living. Other than Franny's efforts, I was making my own calls. I'm not blaming anyone; I made myself difficult to be around for a few years.

Steve had reached out a couple times, but I didn't want to see him during this time of my life. I didn't want him to interfere with what I thought was helping me. I wanted to be with my friends. Well, who I thought were my friends. I wanted to drink; I wanted to get high. I didn't want Steve around, shoving Jesus down my throat. Anytime I would see him, it was the same thing; he would use it as an opportunity to bring up what God could do in my life. I would shut him right down. I'd say, "I don't want that in my life. I'm doing well right now." I had money, I had booze, I had my drugs, I had my wife whenever I wanted her. That was what my mindset was like. I didn't show her the respect she deserved. Most times, I wasn't showing anybody respect. I only cared about myself and what I needed to get through the day.

I noticed Steve was trying to get more involved in my life. I think it's because he was growing concerned for my well-being and the well-being of my marriage. Franny had reached out to him many nights, worried that I wasn't home from the bar yet. Without hesitation, Steve would get in his car, pick up Fran, and they would go to the different bars searching for me to drag me home.

I started to catch on to what they were doing, so I made sure people at the bar kept an eye out for them. There were times they would pull up out front and someone would run inside to let me know. I'd book it out the back door, wait for them to go inside the bar, get in my car and head to the next bar. I didn't want to go home; I didn't want to see my brother; I just wanted to do my own thing. I wasn't ready to go home yet.

It got to the point where I sometimes found myself at the bar at eleven in the morning. I had the day off, so I knew where I wanted to spend it. I sat on the bar stool and just kept on hammering glasses of liquor back. I could barely see my own hands in front of me, let alone the person beside me. Life was blurry. I didn't know where to go from here. When I started thinking like that, I'd order another round of shots and kept on falling further down the black hole beneath me. Pain was my partner, and he was pushing me to buy more drinks. I sat there all day long, until three a.m., and drank. It was a fourteen-hour drinking binge. I don't know how many bars I ended up going to, but they all looked the same by the evening: dark, dim and black.

I got so hammered that night; I have no idea how I got home. All I remember is Franny screaming at me when I came through the door. She wasn't going to take this much longer. Even though I should have passed out from all the drinks, I had trouble sleeping that night. When I woke up, Fran had gone to work and I was all alone in the house. I just sat up in my bed for a few hours and thought about everything I had done. That day it was all hitting me for some reason. I was thinking about how horribly I'd treated my wife, how I'd neglected my brothers and how I'd ignored my parents.

I was trying to find my own way this whole time. I knew the path I was paving was an unsustainable, dark road. For the past half a year, I had this unrelenting knocking going on in my brain about God. My brother would talk about God, my dad would bring up the Bible, and I had been desperately ignoring it. The more I tried to ignore it, the louder the knocking would become. As I was sitting there in my bed listening to the knocking that morning, I remembered the first Bible verse I had ever memorized as a kid: "Behold, I stand at the door, and knock: if any man hears my voice, and open the door, I will come in to him, and will sup with him, and he with me."

I shook my head and tried to ignore my heart again. I was confused, but I was unsure if I really wanted to change. When you have lived your life a certain way for an extended period of time, it's hard to shake the habits. But I knew I had to try something.

So that day, I waited for Franny to come home and I apologized for the night before. This was something that occurred often, so I guess you could say they were pretty empty apologies. I knew I wasn't going to be going out that night, but she was still giving me the cold shoulder. She was asking me questions about the day before. I didn't really feel like answering any questions, so I laid low for the rest of the evening.

At about two o'clock in the morning, I woke up out of a dead sleep and immediately started bawling my eyes out. Franny woke up and comforted me. She had no idea why I was crying, but she was there for me. I told her, "I need to leave. I need to go see my brother."

I stood outside Steve's house, just knocking and crying, hoping he would wake up and open the door. Eventually, I heard the door unlock, and Steve found me standing there with all my emotions on display. "I need to talk to you, Steve."

He opened the door. "Come on in, brother."

We sat down. I didn't even know where to begin. "I've made some bad decisions in my life and I don't know how to repair it. I know I need Jesus in my life and I know I need to be forgiven. That's why I'm here. I want to ask him into my life. I want him to help me get through whatever it is I'm going through. I need him to take control of my life because I can't control it by myself."

I knew Steve could guide me through this process of becoming saved. When I woke up that night, the knocking was the loudest it had ever been. It was telling me to go to my brother's house. This time instead of ignoring the knocking, I opened the doors to my heart.

Steve told me it was easy; I just needed to pray and ask for Jesus to come into my life. "God will forgive you, Jamie. If you want to pray, let's pray together." There was only silence for a good half a minute, and then I was able to muster up the courage to begin praying. I would begin weeping between my sentences. It was very emotional for me. It was a very raw moment. I felt like I was unloading years and years of baggage onto the floor of my brother's house, but more importantly, in front of the throne of my new Lord and Savior. I had known him all my life, but I needed to go through turmoil in order to soften my heart and allow him to take control of my lost soul. Sometimes you just need to hit a crossroads during life's travels in order to push you in the right direction.

I felt the weight of a million sins hamper me down for so long. In that moment, I knew I was forgiven because all the weight pushing me down had eased off my shoulders, and I felt reborn. Jesus saved me.

When I got home, the first thing I said to Franny was, "God has forgiven me. I hope you can forgive me too." We talked through everything, and I made sure she knew how sorry I was and that I was going to give it my full effort to make the necessary changes. I wanted her to know we were going to get through this together. She wasn't fighting this alone anymore; I was going to start fighting as well.

I called my dad and told him what I had been going through and what I had done that night at Steve's. He came and picked me up that same day and took me to a detox center. I spent three days at the center, draining all the booze from my system. From there, the healing process started. Not everything changed right away; it took time. It was a tough process for sure. I still had days where I'd find myself back in the bars, but I had been building a foundation and I was able to bounce back. I was dedicated to change.

I have never been even close to a perfect human being, because I am not worthy. But what Jesus did for me on the cross, shedding his blood and breaking his body, I now have the victory. I am forgiven. I have salvation.

Just because I asked the Lord to come into my life doesn't mean I lead a perfect life. It's an everyday struggle for me. I still make mistakes, I still have my flaws, but I have hope and direction now. I may break, but I am no longer broken. I may get lost sometimes, but I know I am forever found. I know I will never be a perfect person, but it's not about being a perfect person. If humans were perfect, there would be no need for God. I need God.

I stood at my brother's door, I knocked, and he let me in. I laid it all on the line to him. He told me what I had to do. I needed to ask Jesus into my life. So I stood at Jesus's door, riddled with fear, knocking. He welcomed me in with open arms.

Here I am! I stand at the door and knock. If anyone hears My voice and opens the door, I will come in and eat with that person, and they with me.

—Revelation 3:20

CHAPTER XVI
Andiamo

Present Day

The tape reached its end and, as everything flooded back to me, I soaked it all in. Watching the fight again brought back all the memories I had been pushing deep down for way too long. As I sat on the floor in front of my coffee table, I couldn't help but feel troubled. Not only did I go down memory lane in Seoul, but I kept walking and found myself in the bars. I let everything that happened to me in boxing affect my life outside of the ring. I'm lucky Fran loved me and wanted to stick by me during those awful years I put her through. She is the definition of a rock.

Maybe it wasn't so much that I was scared about what the boxes contained, but maybe it was more about what my heart contained. I have never fully gotten over what happened to me in Korea. I left for the Olympics feeling one way and came back a completely different man. I felt broken beyond repair. The voices in my head were yelling at me, but I could never understand what they were saying to me. I followed the blurry path of lies, instead of seeking a truth, because the path of destruction was easier.

It would have been easier to get drunk, throw away all the boxes and continue living life without closure. But I chose to watch the video because I knew I had to. I can't even explain the anxiety I felt pressing play on the video. Watching every punch, every step and every telegraphed movement that took me right back into the ring that day. Every time the Mongolian popped me with a good shot, I felt it. Every time the ring shook as one of us hit the canvas, I felt it. The powerful beating of my heart pulsating through my chest as I realized, yet again, that the ref had ended the match, I felt it. I felt it all.

I watched it, though. I relived my entire boxing career, and I made it straight through to the end. And you know what? I'm okay. It's something I've never said out loud, but I'll say it now: I'm okay. I'm still standing here today; I'm still alive. No matter how difficult it seems in the moment, I ended up being okay. When I got the cut over my eye or when I broke my hand against Kelcie Banks, everything healed up and I pressed forward. Even after my mentor, my coach and one of my best friends had broken my trust and broke my heart into pieces, I picked up those pieces and eventually I made it through to the other side. When I was handed the most controversial decision in Olympic history and left to deal with the aftermath alone, I may have slipped down a steep mountain, but eventually, with the help from the ones who cared about me the most and my faith in Jesus, I began to climb back up.

Through everything I faced, I overcame it. Do I still deal with negative thoughts and emotions on a regular basis? Absolutely. But trust me, I'm in a much better place than I could be. I'm okay. I've been blessed with a beautiful wife and two incredible children. It's not about me anymore; it's about them. It's about helping them navigate through their lives and their struggles, being there for them when they need me. It's all right to reminisce about the great accomplishments I've achieved, but I can't live my whole life in the past. There's a point where you have to move forward and look ahead to what's still to come in life.

My life didn't end at the 1988 Olympics; it was just a moment in time that occurred during my twenty-second year on this earth. I've had thirty years since then to set new goals, achieve new things and write my next chapter. But I haven't. I chose to ride on my past achievements and let that wave carry me. It didn't always carry me to good places, but I thought it was all I had. I hope I didn't waste the last thirty years feeling sorry for myself.

My Olympics are a distant memory, but that doesn't mean I can't create a new Olympics for myself. Just because I'm in my fifties doesn't mean I still can't accomplish new goals. I still have so much life ahead of me. Age is only a number.

Even though I thought looking through these boxes would be damaging, I feel like I've faced the demons that have haunted me and am finally ready to move past my past. I only have the future ahead of me, and I should focus on enjoying the moments I have yet to make. My path hasn't been set in stone; I still have the tools to carve out whatever future I want.

I pack up my boxes with a smile on my face—a smile I haven't felt come across me in quite some time. I am at peace with boxing, and I am at peace with myself. I shouldn't use my story as an excuse to live recklessly. My story should be used to inspire people. No matter how deep of a hole you feel like you're in, you are never alone.

I pick up Steve's boxes and walk them upstairs so I can put them in a special spot because my brother holds a special spot in my heart. He is my big brother and a man I truly look up to and respect. We both accomplished such great things in the sport of boxing. During our careers, we both had our rivalries, we both had our disappointments, we both received many accolades. But through it all, the only things that we still have are some dusty trophies and each other. I love my brother.

Even though it's the middle of the night and I know Fran is sleeping, I send her a text. I tell her how much I love and appreciate every single thing she does for our family. I tell her to give Victoria and Tanner a hug from Dad and to tell them I can't wait to see them when they get home in a couple days. I love my family with all my heart.

The last box I pick up is my own. When I picked it up earlier it felt heavy, but now it feels as light as a feather. I have some of my old boxing memorabilia in the garage, so that's where I'm going to store my boxes. I turn on the light and the first thing I see is Rocky Balboa staring at me from the far wall. I move a couple things around and put my boxes in a safe spot. As I continue to reorganize, I see my old boxing shoes and gloves. They look like they could tell a few stories. I pull them out and try on the shoes. I begin bouncing around a little on my toes. They're a little tight, but they still somehow fit after all these years.

The gloves slide on and my hands feel at home. I smack my hands together to hear the beautiful sound of leather echo through the garage. In the dimly lit garage, at four in the morning, the champ is back. I hit the heavy bag with all my favorite combinations as I picture dropping my opponents to one knee with vicious liver shots. Sweat dripping off the tip of my nose splashes to the floor as I move around the bag picking my spots. I have no music on, but I can hear "Thunderstruck" by AC/DC playing through my head as I feel my hands getting faster and more powerful with each strike of the bag. I throw one final punch to the center of the heavy bag that rattles the entire garage ceiling, sending small pieces of dust and concrete floating in the air toward the ground.

As I leave my garage, I tie the laces of my boxing shoes together and hang them over a nail in the wall. My shoes and my gloves dangle over my box, with a fresh layer of sweat soaking the interior. Boxing will always be a part of my DNA, but now I choose to let go of the negativity, and let my gloves and shoes sway over the memories of the career I take pride in.

Finals Thoughts

You know, it's kind of a cool thing; Steve won his first match at the Olympics, and anyone who has two eyes and half a brain could see he won the second match against the Irishman. I got my Olympic match overturned to show me as the victor, but never competed again. Technically, Steve and I are the only Olympic boxers in history to go undefeated in the Olympics and not win a medal: 3 and 0, baby!

We had so much support during our careers from our wives, our parents, Hank and our family and friends. We were so blessed to have been able to live out such an adventurous dream. Both years we attended the Olympics, Steve and I were the only married men on the team with full-time jobs. To top it all off, Steve had kids at home too. Trying to work the proper amount of training around full-time jobs takes an immense amount of discipline. But it also takes patience and understanding from our families. Without the freedom to do that, we wouldn't have been able to succeed. Franny and Debbie gave Steve and I peace of mind. They never made us feel guilty; they only supported us, even when it was tough. They are the real fighters. Our gold medals are getting to be with such amazing women.

Do I regret anything that happened in my boxing career? No. My boxing career was a lot like life. Life is a learning experience with many ups and downs along the way. You'll achieve your victories, but you'll also face your defeats. You'll shed tears of joy and tears stemming from disappointment. There will be times where you give up in life, but it's all about how you pick yourself up off the canvas. You grow as an athlete and a competitor, much like you grow up from an adolescent into an adult. You learn from your shortcomings and turn weakness into strength. I suffer from mental illness, and it's tough to talk about. but you can never give up. Even when I feel engulfed by darkness, I just pray and continue to search for my light. Find your light. Don't be afraid to talk about how you're feeling. You can always find someone who will want to listen and help you if you need it.

People will try to tear you down as you go through life, for many different reasons. Whether it be jealousy, anger, competitiveness, pettiness or insecurity, life always puts your back up against the ropes. I've learned in both boxing and in life that when your back is up against the ropes, you have to keep fighting. You have to fight for your beliefs, you have to fight for your family, and you have to fight for yourself.

Jamie Pagendam eventually resurrected his boxing career five years after being out of the sport, and recaptured the Canadian Light Welterweight Championship. That same year, he would represent his country in the Commonwealth Games and end his boxing career on his own terms in 1994

Made in the USA
Middletown, DE
15 October 2023

40671790R00182